SURVIVAL/ FIGHTING KNIVES

SURVIVAL/ FIGHTING KNIVES

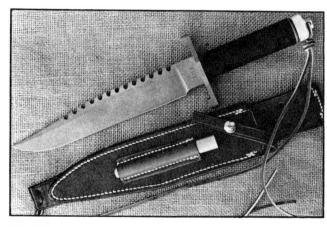

LEROY THOMPSON

PALADIN PRESS
BOULDER, COLORADO

Survival/Fighting Knives
by Leroy Thompson
Copyright © 1986 by Leroy Thompson

ISBN 0-87364-347-x
Printed in the United States of America

Published by Paladin Press, a division of
Paladin Enterprises, Inc., P.O. Box 1307,
Boulder, Colorado 80306, USA.
(303) 443-7250

Direct inquiries and/or orders to the above address.

Contents

1. The Knife as Tool and Weapon 1

2. Utility or General-Purpose Knives 5

3. Commercial Hollow-Handled Survival Knives 23

4. Custom-Made Hollow-Handled Survival Knives and Substitutes 37

5. Survival Knives and Kits 53

6. Folding General-Purpose and Survival Knives 59

7. Fighting Knives 69

8. Street Survival Knives 85

Appendix: Knife Makers 95

1.
The Knife as Tool and Weapon

The composition of the knife—one of man's oldest and most useful tools—has evolved from stone to bronze, iron, steel, stainless steel, or other alloy. Even knives made of plastic are on the market today. Although frequently used as a weapon during its long history, the knife is too versatile to be used for such a function alone; it is, of course, a tool and utensil as well.

The type of knife used and the type and composition of its blade vary in different cultures. Europeans, for example, have traditionally had an affinity for the dagger or poniard, while Americans are most closely associated with Bowie knives and push daggers. The Japanese classic knife is the *tanto*, while the Malaysians have always favored the *kris*. In the Middle East, the *jambiya* is the traditional knife, but up toward the Khyber Pass, the *charas* is still seen tucked into the belts of Afghan freedom fighters. On Afghanistan's borders, the Indians have traditionally used the *khanjar*, though in Nepal, the Ghurkas swear by the *kukri*. Across the border in the Soviet Union, the Cossacks struck fear into the hearts of their enemies with their *kindjal*. These and other traditional edged weapons are interesting, and many are quite useful when employed skillfully.

Rather than examine the history of the knife, *Survival/Fighting Knives* is meant to be a guide for determining which type of knife—even the specific make and model—is most suitable for the reader's individual needs. I make no claim to the completeness of this book, however. On the contrary, though I've tried to evaluate a reasonable number of knives, I've stuck to those with which I've had firsthand experience (with a few exceptions) and which I know to be of acceptable quality and design.

Note that because I have not included some custom-maker's knife, I do not mean to imply such a knife is not an excellent product. I am only concerning myself herein with knives that I have put to the test to determine their acceptability. An important point on custom knives, in fact, is that they are only better than a production knife in certain situations. For example, if a high-quality production knife is available which perfectly suits one's needs, why spend the time and money on a custom blade? The advantage of the custom knife is that one can have it designed exactly to fit one's own usage, and with a skilled and reputable cutler one can count on rigorous quality control.

I should also point out that I am not a professional outdoorsman who spends most of his life up the Amazon. However, I have, both in Vietnam and elsewhere, served with special operation units and have used the knife as a tool—and weapon—in many parts of the world. Still, my views are colored by the fact that I like comfort and look for it wherever I can find it. That doesn't mean that when I've had to lie virtually motionless for hours on an ambush I haven't been able to do so, but I would rather have been lying on a comfortable sofa watching a movie! If time and the situation allow, I try to make the most comfortable camp possible consistent with traveling light.

My recommendations, then, are often based on those knives which have made easier any task I've had to perform. As a result, this book is really not intended for the knife collector as much as it is intended for the man who really uses his knife or knives. He may not use them every day or even every month, but when he needs them, he *really* does need them.

A Ghurka sharpens his kukri. Although a formidable blade, the kukri is also used as a utility blade. Photo courtesy of the Imperial War Museum.

This Spanish fighting/utility knife is used by Spanish special operations troops.

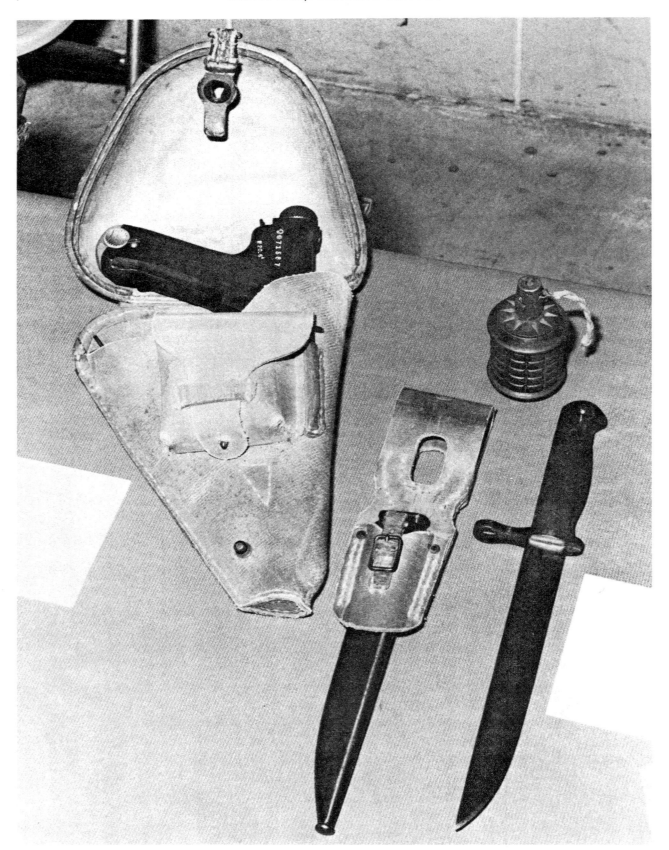

This short bayonet, carried by Japanese paratroopers during World War II, served as both a utility and combat knife.

2.
Utility or General-Purpose Knives

It would be a gross inaccuracy to say that the utility knife is never used as a combat blade. On the contrary, many utility blades—the Ka-Bar is an excellent example—have "done in" their share of the enemy. The utility knife was not, however, intended just for close-quarters combat. Its primary function is either to act as a tool for a specific purpose or to act as a general-purpose implement around the camp or bivouac.

One of the best-known utility blades is the Ghurka kukri, a boomerang-shaped knife. An incredibly useful tool, the kukri is used to chop wood, cut bamboo, chop up meat, cut rope, and decapitate enemies; not necessarily in that order and not limited to these functions alone. The Ghurka's skill with the kukri is so well known that Argentine soldiers surrendered in droves in the Falklands rather than face the "head-hunting mercenaries"—the label applied to the Ghurkas by Argentine propaganda. Yet, despite his vaunted skill in battle with the kukri, the Ghurka considers it to be his primary tool and uses it as such. Westerners sometimes have trouble at first getting the hang of the wrist action necessary to use the kukri most effectively; once mastered, however, the kukri can be wielded with devastating force.

One of the more interesting examples of a knife designed for utility use—but which performed well as a combat blade—was the Renaissance gunner's stiletto. This dagger had graduations along the blade which could be used in measuring charges, while its sharply pointed blade could be used to clear a touch hole or cut a fuse, as well as to deal with an enemy at close quarters. Other stilettos from the same period doubled as a pair of dividers, thus increasing their utility.

The German Red Cross Hewer of World War II is a good example of a knife which served well in the utility role but was not very effective in combat. This heavy knife was purposely manufactured with a blunt point so that the Red Cross men would not appear to be bearing arms. Still, it was equipped with a very useful saw blade (for cutting splints) and a heavy-duty hacking edge.

The U.S. Army has had its share of interesting general-purpose knives as well. The 1890 Entrenching Knife, for example, which had a heavy 8-1/2-inch long and 2-inch wide blade, could be used for everything from digging a foxhole to preparing foraged meat.

It's not surprising that the utility knife has been popular throughout history since man normally devotes far more time to food and shelter and other chores than to killing others, despite what the pessimists may say. Among more current utility knives, a few stand out above the rest.

KA-BAR

The Ka-Bar is a classic among utility knives. Although there are many variations of the Ka-Bar, the one issued to untold numbers of Marines during the last forty-five years is the one that is the most recognizable. With its 7-inch parkerized clipped-point blade and serrated leather washer handle, it is probably the most widely known U.S. military knife.

The Ka-Bar isn't as sturdy as a lot of custom utility knives, but it is very durable. The blade has often been snapped when used too forcefully to pry or puncture, but a lot of Ka-Bars have been used to do both without breaking. The Ka-Bar's forte is performing a lot of tasks reasonably well. The Marines certainly love the

Ka-Bar and don't seem inclined to get rid of it, and that's a pretty solid recommendation. When it comes to doubling as a combat knife, the Ka-Bar has probably accounted for more dead enemy troops than any other American fighting knife. It should be noted, by the way, that "Ka-Bar" has become somewhat of a generic term, and the same basic knife has been made by PAL, Camillus, and Robeson Shuredge as well as Ka-Bar itself.

A general-purpose knife developed for the OSS and SOE in World War II was this copy of the German "gravity knife." The Commandos who were issued this knife learned to kill using the spike to thrust into the carotid artery.

The kukri's design allows it to be wielded with great force.

A member of the U.S. Army Special Forces wears a utility knife of undetermined type on his right hip while serving "survival foods" to VIPs.

Members of the U.S. Army's 77th Special Forces Group (Airborne) put their utility knives to good use preparing meat.

This survival knife, used by the British Army, offers a heavy, durable blade and a comfortable hilt. It is used primarily by troops in Arctic situations.

A member of Merrill's Marauders during World War II wears what appears to be a Ka-Bar utility knife along with his .45 auto.

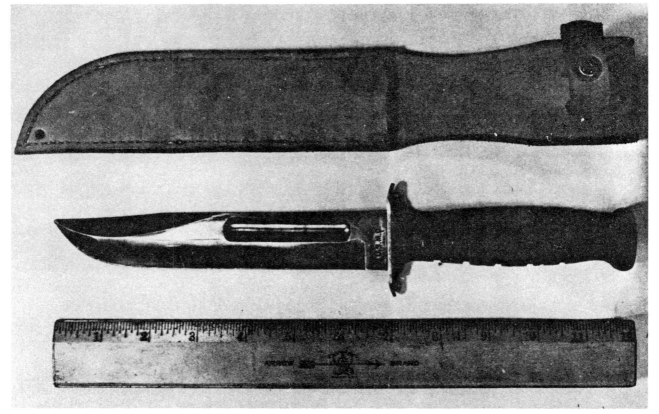

The Marine's old standby, the Ka-Bar. Photo courtesy of the U.S. Marine Corps.

This variation of the Ka-Bar is used by the U.S. Navy SEALs as a utility knife.

JET PILOT'S SURVIVAL KNIFE

Bearing some similarities to the Ka-Bar is the "Jet Pilot's Survival Knife." Despite the fact that this knife was originally designed to be a pilot's knife, it has seen wide usage among other military personnel who value its excellent qualities. It was very popular, for example, with Special Operations Group recon teams in Vietnam, and strike teams of the USAF Combat Security Police often carried this type of survival knife.

The original pilot's survival knife, developed by the Navy in conjunction with Marbles Arms in 1957, had a 6-inch Bowie-style, blued blade with saw teeth along the top. In 1962, however, the blade was shortened to 5 inches, which is the length still in use. Normally, the 5-inch blades have also been parkerized. Like the Ka-Bar, the Jet Pilot's Knife uses stacked leather washers for the handle. The butt plate consists of heavy steel and is designed for pounding or grinding. The crossguard is rectangular in shape and is drilled for a wrist thong.

The leather sheath has a pocket for the sharpening stone which comes with the knife. There are holes in the sheath so that it can be lashed to webbed gear or affixed to a pilot's survival vest. On current sheath models, a sheet-metal reinforcing plate acts as a chape and runs up the back of the sheath.

The Jet Pilot's Survival Knife is intended to be a mass-produced, inexpensive, military utility knife, a function it fulfills admirably. (Of the currently available military utility knives, it is one of my favorites.) Various companies have had the contract to make Jet Pilot's Survival Knives: Camillus, Milpar, Utica, and Ontario (in addition to Marbles) come to mind. My current Jet Pilot is an Ontario made in 1980. There are cheap imitations of this knife around, so you would be well-advised to acquire one made for the military or a military overrun.

A U.S. Ranger advisor to the Viet Rangers wears a Jet Pilot's Survival Knife on his left hip. Photo courtesy of the U.S. Army.

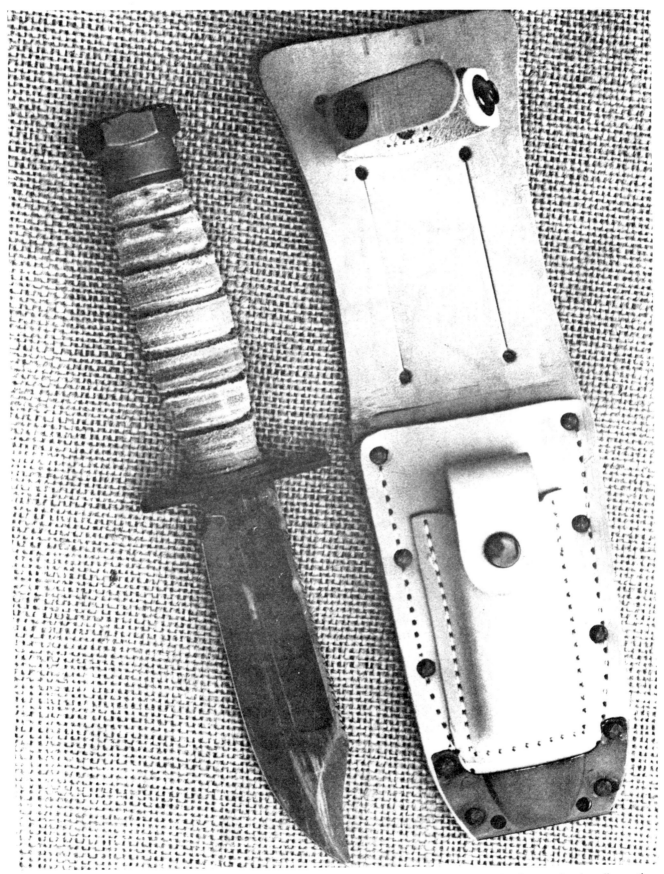

The Jet Pilot's Survival Knife and its sheath. Note the metal chape on the sheath and the leather washer handle on the knife.

Used by U.S. Navy personnel, including the SEALs, the
Mark 3, Model O utility knife shows an extremely
clipped point and a serrated top used to cut rope.

MARK 3, MODEL O

The U.S. Navy uses another utility knife known as the Mark 3, Model O. This well-made knife has a 6-inch, blued-steel blade with a pronounced clipped point and rope-cutting serrations along the top edge. The crossguard is also blued steel and is shaped in an elongated diamond. Grip scales are of high-impact plastic and are heavily checkered with "USN" molded in. The steel butt is flat so that it can be used for pounding. The butt cap is also drilled for a wrist thong which passes through it.

The Mark 3, Model O's sheath is made of black molded plastic or fiber and has a black webbed frog, which allows the knife to be attached either via a belt loop or a hanger for a pistol belt. The bottom of the sheath is pierced for a tie-down thong.

Although the extremely clipped point bothers me since it is somewhat fragile, I am otherwise quite impressed with this high-quality knife. It is said that the Navy SEALs are using it, and they have high standards in equipment.

U.S. NAVY UNDERWATER KNIFE

Speaking of knives used by the SEALs, the U.S. Navy Underwater Knife is a utility knife designed for specialized usage. Made of a nonferrous alloy, this knife has a 7-1/4-inch parkerized blade with saw teeth along the back of the blade. The scales and sheath are of high-impact plastic. This seems to be a durable and functional knife from the examples I've examined, though it has made the news as one of those boondoggles which cost the government a ridiculous price to replace.

MACHETES

Although not strictly knives, machetes can often function as good utility blades when used properly. Like the really heavy-duty survival knives, they're normally a bit large to be used with real finesse, however. The "Worldwide Survival Tool" which Brigade Quartermaster lists in its catalog seems to be a useful one. Along with the "Commando Jump Sheath" sold with it,

Even the machete makes a useful general-purpose blade if used with care. Members of the old 77th Special Forces Group are shown using a machete to cut meat. Photo courtesy of the U.S. Army.

This odd-looking machete was used by the Special Forces in Vietnam and was often used as a heavy-utility cutting implement.

the "Tool" should be a most useful item in the outdoors.

The old "Woodsman's Pal," or as its successor was known in Vietnam, the "Survival Tool Type IV," is another useful heavy-duty utility blade. Of general machete type, this knife in its later version has a heavy 10-inch blade of interesting design. The primary edge is sharpened for cutting and hacking, but it does not have a point. It has more of a cleaver shape with a sharpened hook on the back edge. In Vietnam, this knife functioned primarily as a survival tool carried in choppers, but a few turned up in the hands of grunts.

THE TANTO AND OUTDOORSMAN

Though the Cold Steel Tanto is primarily a fighting knife, its durable 6-inch stainless steel blade and rubberized Pachmayr-style grip have made it relatively popular for utility use. Recently, Cold Steel has added the Outdoorsman to its line. Designed for the utility market, the Outdoorsman has virtually the same hilt and crossguard as the Tanto but has a distinctly different blade, with a more traditional point and blade sweep. There's still a lot of steel at the tip, however, to keep the Outdoorsman's point sturdy. I have used the Tanto more than once to open oil cans, and I certainly wouldn't hesitate to use the Outdoorsman for such cutting either. Along the top (or back) of the blade is a sharpened section about 2 inches long which can be used for hacking, while the back of the blade near the crossguard has serrations.

Both the Tanto and Outdoorsman come with the same well-made sheath, which has a Velcro retaining strap and loops which enable you to wear it on the belt or upside down on combat suspenders.

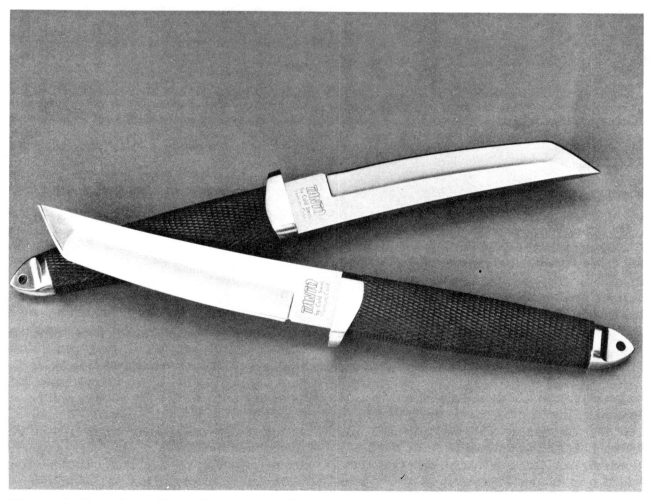

Although the Tanto is usually considered to be a fighting knife, its durability makes it a good utility knife as well. Photo courtesy of Cold Steel.

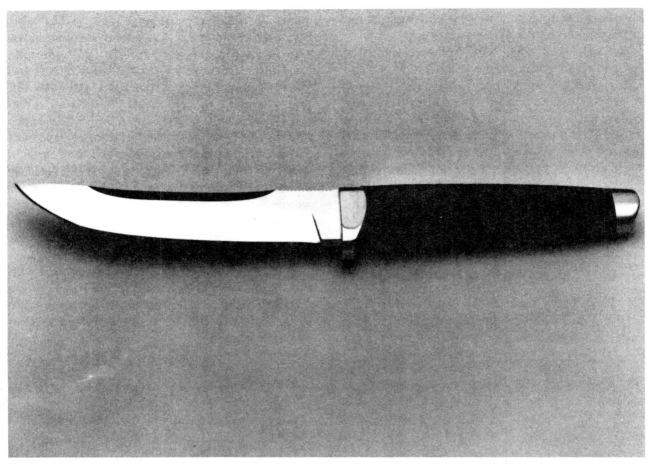

The Cold Steel Outdoorsman is a general-purpose version of the Tanto. Photo courtesy of Cold Steel.

RANDALL KNIVES

Among custom knifemakers, there is a wealth of general-purpose knives, some of which are called "hunting knives." As with all custom knives, one should take advantage of the fact that a custom knife can be tailor-made to one's needs. Frequently, one of the knives discussed in this work under the heading "survival knives" will make an excellent utility knife. In fact, the purpose of a survival knife is to be utilitarian.

My choice of custom-makers for general-purpose military usage is Randall, my favorite fighting/utility knives being the Model 14 "Attack" or Model 15 "Aircrewman." The Model 14 is a heavy-duty knife with a 7-1/2-inch Bowie-style blade and black Micarta handle, which incorporates finger grooves and a brass crossguard. Saw teeth along the top/back of the blade are an option, and I would recommend

them since they add to the knife's utility. I have found this knife to be incredibly durable for field usage, while its shape and balance allow it to double as a fighting knife if needed. The Model 15 is basically the same knife, but with a 5-1/2-inch blade. Many find the shorter blade easier to use for most chores.

For the serving soldier, sailor, airman, or marine, the utility knife is the most likely type of knife to be issued, which along with the hollow-handled survival knife is likely to be the most useful. The utility or survival knife, with its ability to perform a lot of tasks, will be the best choice for the outdoorsman. The primary purpose of any utility knife is that it must adequately perform whatever job it's called upon to do, ranging from skinning a deer to eliminating the enemy at close-quarters. It must also retain the ability to keep performing the job again and again.

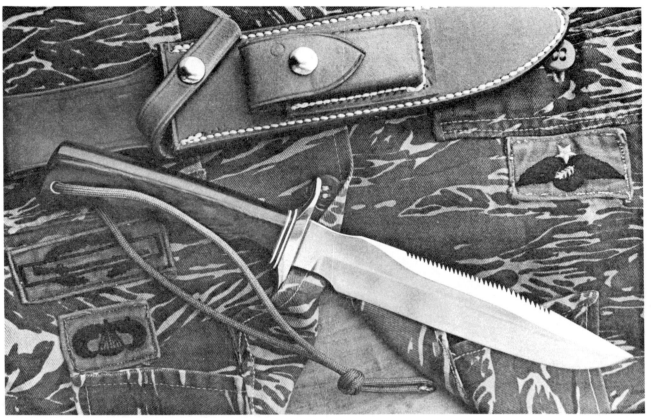

The classic lines of this Randall show why it has always been the fighting man's choice.

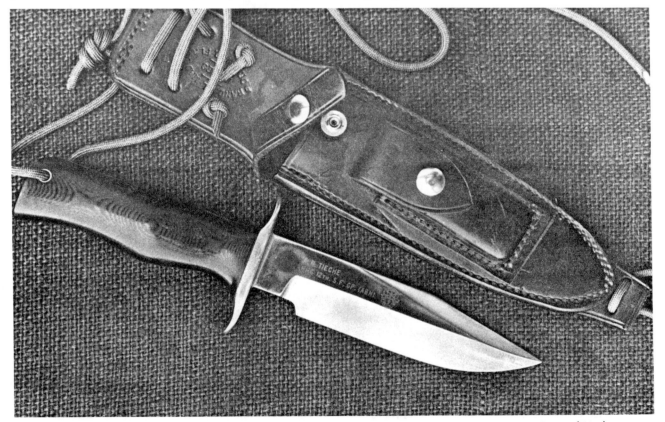

The Randall fighting/survival/general-purpose knife is used by members of the 12th Special Forces Group (Abn).

The Model 14, perhaps today's most popular Randall with military personnel, has a saw-tooth blade, which adds to the knife's utility value.

These two Randalls—the Model 18 at left and the Model 15 at right—saw a lot of use in Vietnam.

3.
Commercial Hollow-Handled Survival Knives

Although the Rambo films seem to have given the hollow-handled survival knife the same appeal that the "Dirty Harry" films granted the S&W Model 29, the concept of a blade with storage space in the hilt is by no means new. In fact, Renaissance swords and daggers occasionally incorporated storage space in either the hilt or the sheath for certain necessities. Actually, the hollow-handled survival knife as it is now known dates back about four decades to knives manufactured by Case and Ka-Bar in the 1940s. The first custom knife of this type to achieve wide popularity was the Randall Model 18 "Attack/Survival," used by many in Vietnam, including myself.

The hollow-handled survival knife has a lot of critics as well as advocates, with myself staunchly among the latter. Some of the criticisms of this type of knife are, however, justified, the most common being that the lack of a full-length tang weakens the knife so that the blade is likely to separate from the hilt during hard usage. Though a valid criticism, recent techniques in joining the shortened tang to the hilt have greatly enhanced the integrity and strength of some hollow-handled knives.

Another common criticism is that the knife is expected to do too much. Individuals purchase a custom hollow-handled knife and think they have a talisman that will enable them to survive—no matter what. Such an attitude is, of course, ridiculous, but the whole point of the hollow-handled knife is that it can perform a wealth of functions in emergency situations. Having such a knife is similar to having an insurance policy should one find himself facing the wilderness with nothing else: obviously, if one anticipates every crisis, one would always be prepared. Of course, on the down side, he'd be

carrying so much gear he'd never get far from civilization anyway. The basic tenet in using the hollow-handled survival knife is that it should be a useful heavy-duty knife in normal guise, but that the kit in its handle is there for last-ditch usage.

Although a lot of people simply like knives and own custom survival knives just for the pleasure of having them, there are certain people who find the hollow-handled survival knife to be especially useful. Almost anyone who works, hunts, or hikes in the boonies should find a good hollow-handled survival knife to be a useful tool and a comforting edge against Murphy's Law of the Jungle, which states that whatever can go wrong will and only the strong and prepared will survive such disasters. Those who work consistently far from civilization—rangers, game wardens, bush pilots, prospectors, and trappers, for example—are all very likely to be customers for a hollow-handled survival knife.

Traditionally, however, the foremost customers for such knives have been military personnel, who by the nature of their profession may have to survive in a hostile environment. In Vietnam, the Randall Model 18 was especially popular with those troops who operated in small units, often in "Indian Country," and were likely to have to "E&E" (Escape and Evade) the enemy if detected. The Army Long Range Reconnaissance Patrol, Special Forces, and Rangers; the Air Force Pararescuemen, Combat Controllers, and Combat Security Police; Marine Recons; Navy SEALs; and chopper pilots were among the users of the Model 18.

Special operations troops around the world justifiably continue to be among the leading customers for such knives. For example, I have seen hollow-handled survival knives carried

Mike England fighting and survival knives, including some miniature hollow-handled knives, are shown above. Photo courtesy of Mike England.

Though not tested by the author, these hollow-handled survivors from Mike England have a sound reputation. Photo courtesy of Mike England.

by the members of the following units: U.S. Army Special Forces, Rangers, and airborne; U.S. Navy SEALs; USAF Pararescuemen; French Foreign Legion; French Regiment Parachute Infantry Marines; French Marine Commandos; Rhodesian Selous Scouts, Special Air Service, and Rhodesian Light Infantry; South African Recce Commandos; Australian Special Air Service; Spanish Special Operations Companies and Spanish Foreign Legion; Sultan of Oman's Special Force; and British Special Air Service.

Because I have at times worked in some Third World countries as an advisor to police or military units, a Randall Model 18—or more recently, a Parrish Combat Survival knife—has often been a companion. As an "advisor" or "trainer," I frequently carried only my knife and a handgun. As a result, it was a comfort to know that my personally selected survival/E&E kit was available in the hilt of the knife and/or secured about my belt in pouches.

Because many of the professionals who carry a survival knife consider it to be a tool which may someday save their lives, they expect a lot from their hollow-handled blade. It is expected to provide shelter, warmth, and food

and be capable of cutting wood and other materials to build fires and construct shelter, cutting snares or materials for traps or nets, skinning game, or spearing fish. The survival-knife owner may also expect it to aid in navigation, provide health care, act as a signaling device, or serve as a weapon. Among the tools or implements the survival knife may have to function as is the spear, hatchet, saw, machete, screwdriver, hammer, chisel, compass, and drill. Depending on the contents of that small compartment in the handle, the knife may also hold supplies for fishing, health care, sewing, and fire-starting.

Obviously, with the myriad of tasks it's expected to perform, the survival knife must be chosen very carefully. With dozens of models on the market—and prices ranging from ten dollars to one thousand dollars—the choice can be bewildering. To help you determine which hollow-handled survival knife to buy, I've compiled the following guide to some of the most commonly encountered knives of this type.

Since the commercial hollow-handled knives are the most readily available and the most widely used, I'll cover them first.

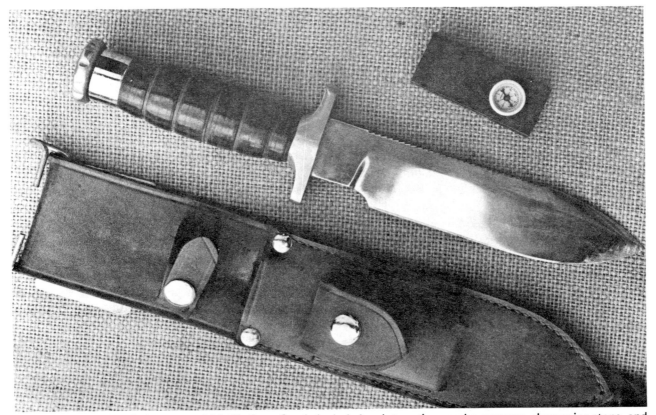

This early hollow-handled commercial knife from Garcia included an interesting combo compass, sharpening stone, and storage compartment which fit into the pouch on the front of the sheath.

LIFEKNIFE

The Lifeknife family of knives has proved highly successful based on its wide availability, its inclusion of a compact survival kit with the knife, and its most reasonable price of $35 to $60 (depending on the model).

Original Lifeknife

The Original Lifeknife has a 6-inch, Bowie-style blade of 420 series stainless steel. This blade is hardened to Rockwell 57-58 and is highly polished so it can also serve as a signal mirror. The top of the blade bears twelve serrations for sawing.

The aircraft aluminum handle is hollow and grooved in "Tootsie-Roll" fashion, being similar to the Ka-Bar in appearance. This handle is blackened and is watertight when sealed with the threaded brass cap which comes with the knife. Actually, two caps come with the knife, one with a liquid-filled luminous compass and one solid one for use in hammering or grinding.

Along with the Lifeknife comes a survival kit inside the handle which includes a wire saw, six feet of snare/utility wire, twenty feet of nylon line, fish hooks, sewing needles, and lifeboat matches. The black leather sheath incorporates a pocket which contains a small sharpening stone.

Commando

My personal favorite among the Lifeknife models is the "Commando." This Lifeknife has a 6-inch, 440-C stainless steel blade with eleven serrations intended to cut wood, sheet metal, or nylon rope. The blade on the Commando is more of a spear-point than a Bowie style, which makes it sturdier for prying and other utility usage. The crossguard is drilled so that the Commando can be lashed to a pole for use as a spearhead.

The hollow handle of the Commando is also of aircraft aluminum but is molded with finger grooves. The same two butt caps are included and seal the storage compartment so that it is watertight using the O-ring included. In addition to the same survival items included with the Original Lifeknife, the Commando also includes sinkers for fishing and a loose compass for use when the solid butt is in place.

The Commando's sheath incorporates two small pockets, one on the front and one on the back. The front one carries the double-sided sharpening stone, while the rear one can be used for carrying additional survival items. The sheath and roughened handle of the Commando are available in either a black or camouflage finish, with the camo adding ten dollars to the price.

Trailmaster

A slightly more compact version of the Lifeknife is the "Trailmaster." Its Bowie-type blade is 5 inches of 440-C stainless steel with serrations that are shallower than the two knives discussed above. The Trailmaster's hollow Valox handle is imprinted on the outside with the International Ground-to-Air Emergency Rescue signals. As with other Lifeknives, the butt cap incorporates a liquid-filled compass. The same basic Lifeknife survival kit, less the wire saw, is included as it is with the other knives. In addition, a small medical kit, which contains a tourniquet, scalpel, suture, antibiotic cream, topical anesthetic, disinfectant, butterfly bandages, salt tablets, aspirin, and other first-aid items, is included.

The medical kit fits into a special pocket on the Cordura nylon sheath. Though a sharpening stone is furnished with the Trailmaster, there is no pocket for it. There is not enough room for it in the pocket which holds the medical kit unless some of the medical items are removed.

Floatknife

For boaters and divers, Lifeknife also offers the "Floatknife," which, as its name indicates, will float if it should fall into the water. The Floatknife's buoyancy is provided by its Dupont Zytel hollow handle, which is yellow for easy visibility. The double-edged 440-C stainless steel blade has serrations along the top for sawing, while the other edge is razor sharp for cutting. A slot cut almost the full length of the blade lowers the weight and aids buoyancy.

The Floatknife's butt cap, also of Zytel, contains a luminous, liquid-filled compass. Imprinted on the handle are both the Morse Code and Emergency Rescue signals. Within the hollow handle is the same basic survival kit found in the Trailmaster. The same compact medical kit included with the Trailmaster is also included in a pocket on the Floatknife's Cordura nylon sheath.

The cammo hilt and sheath of the Lifeknife Commando are shown here, along with the contents of its hollow handle.

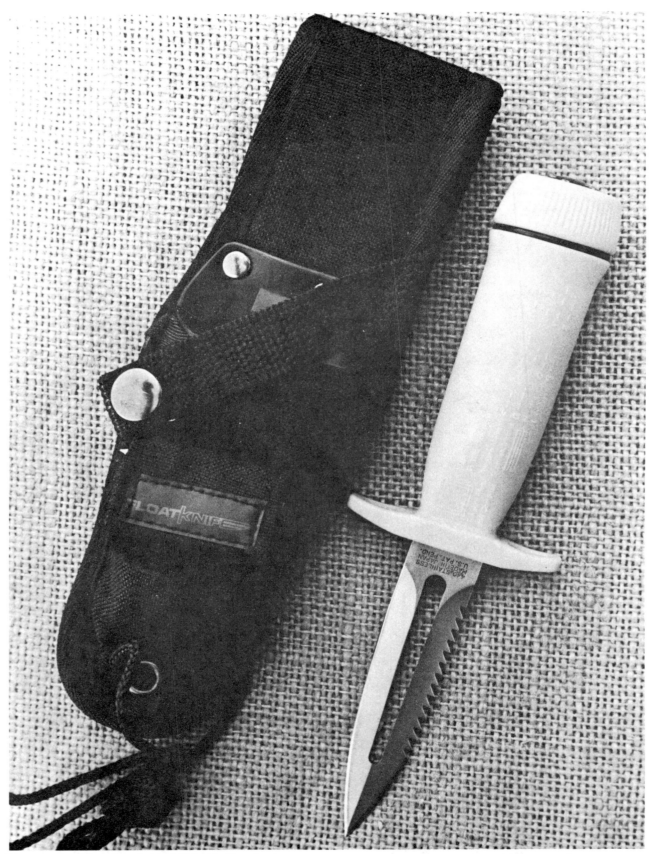

The oversized handle of this Lifeknife Floatknife helps make the knife buoyant and provides a lot of storage space. This knife, with its Cordura nylon sheath, would be a good knife to stow aboard a boat.

A General Note on Lifeknives

Although the Lifeknife line offers excellent value for the money, I would not normally choose one as my primary utility/survival knife which I use virtually every day. Though quite durable, the Lifeknife group of knives will not stand up to some of the same hard usage that the better custom survival knives can tolerate. The Lifeknife is not really intended to be a heavy duty knife, either. It is at its best when employed as a general-purpose outdoors knife by the casual user or when kept in an emergency survival kit in case of need. The latter is, in fact, the task the Lifeknife knives perform best. Because of the well-thought-out survival kits included with the knives and their very reasonable prices, Lifeknives can be bought in multiples and stored for emergency usage. For example, I have two four-wheel-drive vehicles, and I keep a Lifeknife Commando in one and a Trailmaster in the other. Normally, when off-roading I'll have one of my custom knives as well as a firearm and other survival gear along. No matter what my plans may be, a Lifeknife, still in the box with its kit, is permanently stored in the vehicle. I think that it is advisable to keep such a kit in the cabins of light planes or boats, weekend cabins in the woods, or any other place a survival situation could arise. A lot of people just don't have the time or the inclination to assemble their own survival kit, but by purchasing a Lifeknife one then has a kit and basic survival tool in one package. The Lifeknife could also be an excellent addition to one's survival retreat. Three or four Lifeknives not only would make good spares, but they would also be excellent barter material if and when times got very, very bad.

BREWER EXPLORER

I rate the Brewer very highly; it is, in fact, my own favorite among the commercial hollow-handled survival knives. The Brewer's blade is 6-1/2 inches in length, and it is fabricated of 440-C stainless steel which has been black-chromed. On some models the blade is polished for use as a signaling mirror. Since the Brewer is a military-type survival knife, which may double in night combat usage, I prefer the blackened blade. Along the top of the blade are twenty-two well-designed saw teeth, which work very well. The teeth, which are the full width of the blade in order to avoid binding, are angled at 35 degrees to avoid clogging. Also incorporated into the blade are a clinometer (for determining the angle of elevation of something from the horizon as an aid to navigation), five International Ground-to-Air signals (assistance, negative, medical, affirmative, and direction), and a six-centimeter ruler. A slot in the blade allows the knife to be used in conjunction with the sheath as a wire cutter. The section of the blade used for wire cutting has even been specially tempered. This same slot can also be used with an optional harpoon barb.

The Explorer's hollow handle is of cast aluminum with a nonslip black epoxy finish and comfortable finger grooves. A removable handguard is incorporated instead of a crossguard. It is useful should the knife be used in hand-to-hand combat or when gripped while being used for such tasks as hammering. The nonmagnetic stainless steel butt cap, which is drilled for a wrist thong, has a built-in compass inside the cap where it is well protected. The compass is liquid-filled and designed to be highly shock-resistant. (When I compared it with my Prismatik compass, it proved quite accurate.)

Inside the hollow handle is a tubular, waterproof plastic container which contains a miniature survival kit. Like the knife itself, the "Survival Capsule" is very well designed, and contains a needle and suture thread, scalpel, sewing needles, magnesium flint bar (fire starter), waterproof and windproof matches and striker, water-purification tablet, and a fishing kit (six hooks, two sinkers, a float, and fishing line) intended to be used by affixing the line through a small hole in the blade. The knife can thus be used as the rod, especially if a shaft has been fitted into the hollow handle to convert the knife into a spear. The Morse code is printed on the outside of the capsule, which is one of the Explorer's foremost features. A similar capsule should be furnished with any hollow-handled knife since it allows one to remove the survival items without dumping them out piecemeal, thereby preventing the loss of a precious aspirin, water-purification tablet, or fish hook.

The Explorer's sheath is also well designed and functional. Fabricated of glass-fiber rein-

The **Brewer Explorer** with its survival capsule, compass, and sheath. Note the clinometer on the blade and the cutout for use with wire cutters.

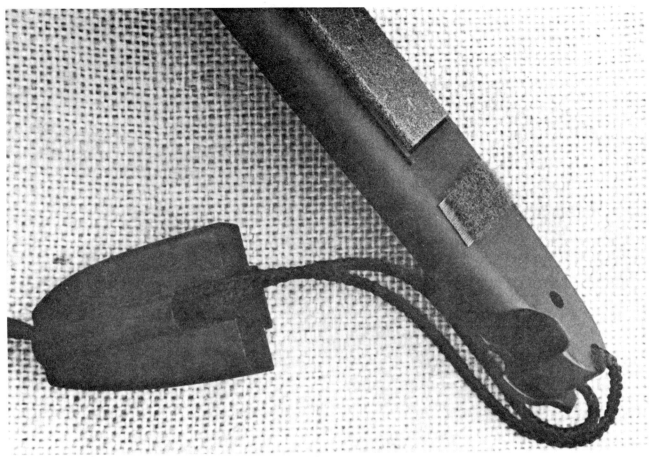

The tip of this Brewer Explorer's sheath can act as a wire cutter in combination with the knife.

forced Poliamid with a webbed belt loop and sharpening stone built into the back of the sheath, it is one of the best available for a survival knife. When the protective cap at the base of the sheath is pulled downward, the wire-cutter pivot and a screwdriver blade are exposed. The tie-down thong keeps the sheath from falling off.

The current list price of the Brewer Explorer is about $150, and I consider it a real bargain at that price. I especially recommend it for military usage since it incorporates many features which should prove useful for battlefield, bivouc, and SERE (Survival, Escape, Resistance, Evasion). Of commercial hollow-handled survival knives, this is my personal top choice.

JUNGLE KING

Like the Brewer Explorer, the Aitor Jungle King is manufactured in Toledo, Spain, a tradi-tional center of quality blades. The Jungle King has a 5-1/2-inch, blackened stainless steel blade with a sturdy spear point. Saw teeth, which run about 2-1/2 inches along the top of the blade, are full width and angled with staggered teeth to reduce binding or clogging. Overall, the blade design is effective, but it is a light blade which lacks the weight needed for hacking or some other heavy uses.

The hilt is of black anodized aluminum alloy with knurled bands to enhance its ability to be gripped. There is a small hole in the hilt's base where a roll pin passes through the hilt, cross-guard, and blade. The blade is sweated into the hilt about an inch inside the crossguard, thereby making the knife relatively sturdy as hollow-handled knives go. The lack of a full-length tang, however, is still one of the disadvantages of such knives. The crossguard has a hole on each side which, combined with the hole through the hilt, should allow the knife to be effectively lashed to a pole that is thrust into the handle cavity.

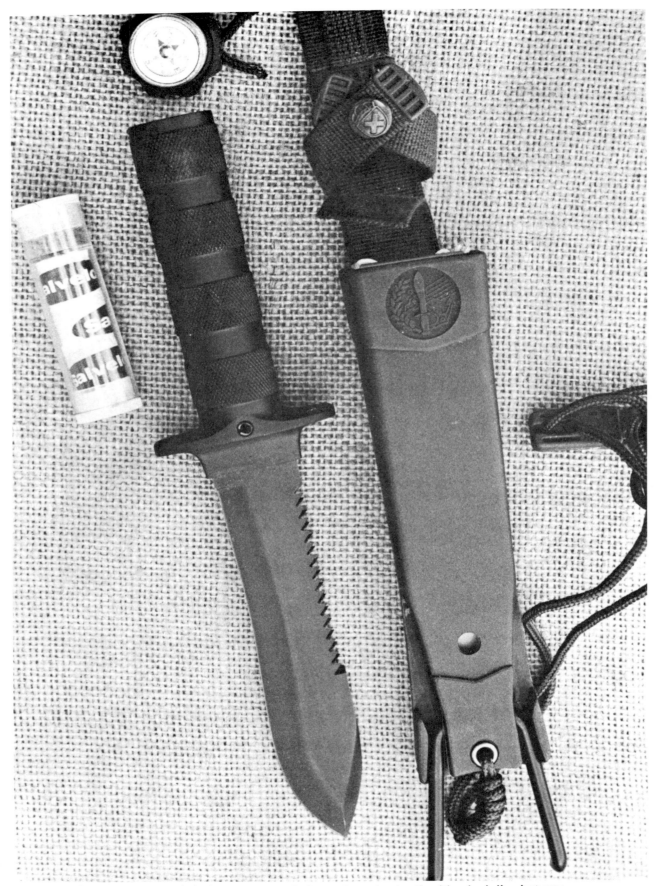

The Jungle King has a compass in its butt cap, a survival capsule, and a sheath with raised slingshot ears.

The butt cap is also made of aluminum and has a hole through which a wrist thong is affixed. Inside the butt cap is a rather cheap compass which is not liquid-filled. Still, it is better than no compass, assuming one has checked its accuracy and bears in mind its margin of error. It should at least serve as an emergency backup to a larger, more sophisticated compass. I always view the compass on a survival knife as a backup in any case.

Like the Explorer, the Jungle King incorporates a "survival capsule." In one respect I like this one even better than that of the Explorer. The Jungle King's 2-3/4-inch-long capsule has two compartments—one large one which contains the "Kit" and one small one for carrying water-purification tabs, aspirins, "uppers," etc. The survival kit packed in the other compartments contains three fish hooks, sinkers, about three meters of fishing line, a small pencil, two safety pins, two needles, thread, a scalpel, tweezers, two Band-Aids, and a flint for starting fires.

The Jungle King's sheath not only carries the knife, but it offers a wealth of additional survival gear. The sheath itself is of olive drab, high-impact plastic and has a very wide mouth, the purpose of which will become clear shortly. The belt loop is of olive drab webbing, and there is also an olive drab tie-down thong. Built into the back of the sheath is a sharpening stone. I should note here that I consider the incorporation of the sharpening stone into the sheath an excellent idea since you are less likely to lose the stone and it is easier to use, being so accessible.

At the base of the sheath, where the chape would be located, are two arms which fold out from the sheath at 180 degrees, forming a slingshot. To complete assembly of the slingshot, one must remove a metal frame/holder which fits into the back half of the sheath's mouth. Wrapped around this frame is latex tubing (including a pouch for the projectile) which can be affixed to the arms of the sheath, thereby forming the slingshot. This latex tubing can also double as a tourniquet. Though not as effective as some of the excellent commercial slingshots available, the one incorporated into the Jungle King will certainly work better than one created from a forked branch and the elastic from one's

The mouth of the Jungle King's sheath, in which one can see the frame which carries a harpoon shaft.

Jockey Shorts! (I should note, by the way, that anyone constructing slingshots using the elastic from Jockey Shorts must bear in mind that it is quite difficult to shoot accurately when you need one hand to hold the slingshot, one to pull back the elastic, and one to hold up your shorts!) I tried the slingshot on the Jungle King using 000 buckshot for ammo and could shoot relatively accurately out to fifteen to twenty yards. It might be a good idea, though, to tape some ammo to the back of the sheath or carry some along with the knife in some other way since stones will not perform as well.

Another useful implement fitted into the frame inside the sheath is a small harpoon blade, which has holes and a line for affixing it to a shaft. Theoretically, this harpoon head is for fishing, but it can also be used to construct spring-and-spear traps. A device which might be even more useful and versatile would be a broad-headed hunting arrowhead. I used to get two or three such arrowheads out of Air Force survival kits in Vietnam and include them in my E&E kit. Bear in mind, though, that you can include just so much gear in the handle and sheath of a knife!

What really adds to the usefulness of the harpoon is that it also incorporates a can opener, bottle opener, screwdriver, and shackle wrench into its design. When using these other tools, be careful so that you don't harpoon your hand. One final implement included in the package is the frame which holds the harpoon and latex tubes. It has a polished section which can be used as a signal mirror. The frame can also serve as a base when constructing certain types of traps or snares.

The overall quality of the Jungle King is not up to that of the Brewer Explorer, but its versatility and low price of about $100 make it a viable choice for some survival tasks. I especially like the inclusion of the slingshot and the harpoon/can-opener tool since both devices could prove to be most useful in a survival situation.

Although I know for a fact that some Spanish special operations units use the Jungle King, I would normally want a heavier-duty knife as my everyday working blade, especially for military use. I would and do use the Jungle King in the same manner as I use the Lifeknife—as an emergency item to be carried or stored in places where I could conceivably need a survival knife. The fact that the Jungle King is so versatile and offers so many functions makes it an excellent knife for inclusion in an off-road vehicle's kit or in a light plane's survival items.

BUCKMASTER

This large, heavy-duty survival knife from Buck Knives is intended to compete with the big custom hollow-handled knives from Lile, Randall, Parrish, and others.

The Buckmaster's 7-1/2-inch, Bowie-style blade has a sandblasted gray finish. Along the top of the blade are nine raker-style saw teeth, while the clipped portion of the blade has nine teeth for sawing rope or nylon cord. Though they are full-blade width to retard bind-ing, the raker saw teeth on this knife are not very effective, requiring a great deal of effort to accomplish anything. The teeth on the clipped edge, on the other hand, are very effective on rope and other heavy line. The blade is heavy enough and balances well for hacking. Since the Buckmaster also has one of the strongest lock-ups between the blade and hilt of any hollow-handled knife, there is little likelihood that the blade will separate from the handle even under hard usage.

The crossguard is very heavily made with a slight "hook" on each side toward the blade. On each side is a threaded hole which can be used to either lash the knife when used as a sur-vival spear or to screw in two "anchors" which come with the knife. Theoretically, these anchors allow the knife to be used as a grappling hook or as some other implement, but I really find they just get in the way when on the knife and do not store anywhere about the sheath conveniently. Hence, I don't use them. The Buckmaster was supposedly designed with cer-tain U.S. Navy units (such as the SEALs) in mind, which may offer some explanation for this feature.

The hollow handle offers a large storage area and hand-filling knurled gripping surface. The butt cap, which has an O-ring to ensure water tightness, contains an internal compass and fits through a large lanyard ring located between the handle and the butt cap.

The Buckmaster's "Griptite" sheath is of black high-impact plastic, with two slots on each side so that it can be strapped to a leg or addi-tional gear can be lashed on. The retaining strap and belt loop are of black webbing, and there is a tie-down thong at the bottom of the sheath. A sharpening stone is incorporated into the back of the sheath. One feature of the sheath that could prove useful is the inclusion of two op-tional pouches (one small, one large) which can be affixed to the sheath to carry more gear. When additional items are attached to the sheath, of course, both bulk and weight are in-creased; therefore you must weigh the advan-tages of additional items on the sheath against having to carry more on the belt.

The Buckmaster is a large knife that has that "First Blood" look without the price of a cus-tom knife. I feel, however, that its more than two pounds of weight legislates against choosing

The odd lugs or anchors of the Buckmaster screw into the crossguard.

it as a general survival/utility knife. Its weight, combined with the saw teeth's relative ineffectiveness would cause me to evaluate the Buckmaster below some of the other commercial knives of this type, especially the Brewer Explorer.

I have by no means covered all of the available commercial hollow-handled knives, but those discussed represent some of the most popular models. More to the point, they represent the models I have used in the field and know to be of acceptable quality.

4.
Custom-Made Hollow-Handled Survival Knives and Substitutes

The wealth of custom hollow-handled survival knives is even greater than that of commercial models. A healthy proportion of custom knifemakers have added a hollow-handled survivor to their product line due to the popularity of the Rambo films and the resulting demand for such knives. Once again, I am not able to evaluate all of the knives available—nor even a majority of them—but I have used some of the most popular custom models, one, in fact, for almost twenty years. The same criteria I have applied to the knives I have tested can also be applied to other knives. Because of the expense involved in buying a custom knife and the potential for having the maker incorporate any special features you may want, be sure to evaluate your needs carefully and select a knife which will serve you for life—as a good custom knife should be expected to do.

There are less well-known custom knifemakers who produce high-quality survival knives; however, bear in mind that the better-known and longer-established custom knifemakers have perfected their designs and must protect their reputations. Since some custom-made knives from established makers have been around for awhile, you can ask the knife owners how well the knives have performed. Another advantage of choosing a knife from one of the better-known custom makers is that examples of their basic models will often be on hand for immediate delivery.

LILE SLY II

This excellent custom knife is the descendant of the custom blade Jimmy Lile produced for Sylvester Stallone for the film *First Blood*. Probably the best single word to describe the Sly II is "impressive." That, of course, is why Sylvester Stallone selected the big Lile knife to be his co-star in *First Blood:* it's an attention-getter.

The Sly II is offered in three blade lengths: 6, 7-1/2, or 9 inches. The 9-inch version is closest to the *First Blood* knife; for all around usage, though, the 7-1/2-inch blade might be more efficient. The Bowie-style blade is made of 440-C stainless steel with a matte finish. Like most survival knives, the Sly II has saw teeth along the top of the blade. The Lile saw teeth are among the most efficient I've tested, working effectively on everything from nylon rope to wood. To give the saw versatility, the first four teeth, which merge into the sharpened clip, are single raker teeth. These teeth taper into the eight unique Lile "split teeth" toward the middle of the blade. The split teeth are the full width of the blade in order to counter binding on wood or bone, while the four narrower raker teeth toward the front of the blade are designed to work well on nylon rope and thin sheeting (such as fiber glass).

Though the Sly II's blade is massive, it is very well-balanced, thereby being a good compromise between general usage and possible combat service. In fact, I give the Sly II's blade very high marks overall, except for the fact that its sharply clipped point might break if used for prying; hence, caution must be used. For other cutting tasks, however, it works marvelously.

The matte stainless-steel crossguard is as massive as one would expect on a knife such as the Sly II. There is the expected hole on each side for lashing the knife to a shaft if used as a spear or for affixing a wrist thong. One feature I especially like on the crossguard are the lugs on each side, which would be useful in combat as a blade catcher while also helping to protect the hand

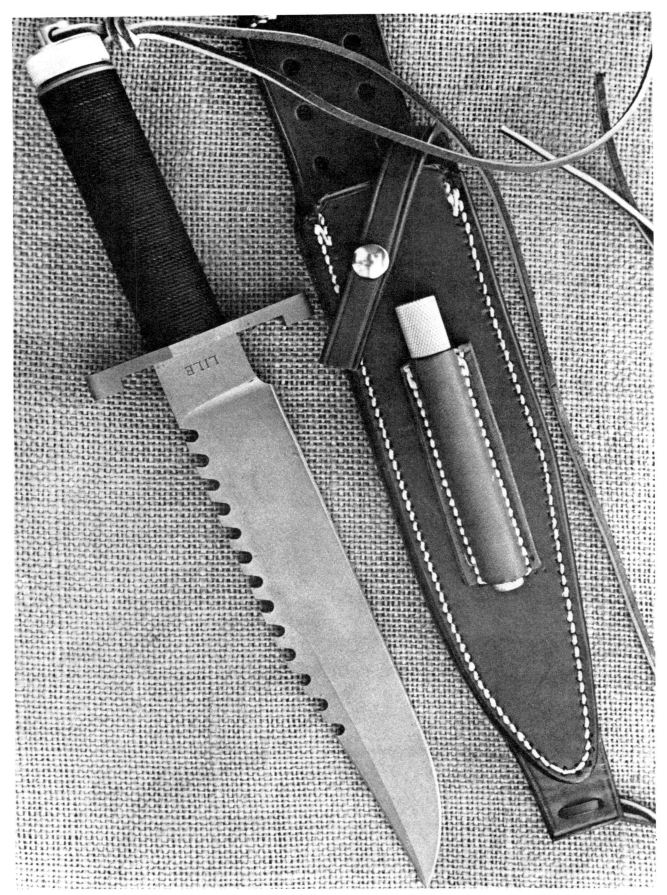

The Lile Sly II with its sheath. Note the line used to wrap the handle/hilt.

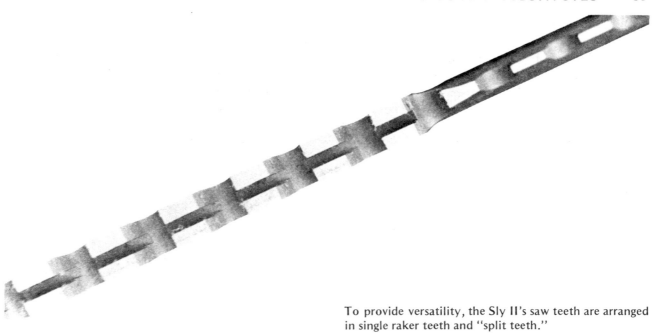

To provide versatility, the Sly II's saw teeth are arranged in single raker teeth and "split teeth."

The Sly II balances very well in the hand whether used in combat or for general-purpose functions.

in utility usage. Even though I like the lugs, though, I'd trade them for the Phillips and blade screwdrivers built into the ends of the cross-guard on the original *First Blood* knife.

The Sly II's 5-inch hollow handle is also made of matte stainless steel and offers a good capacity for storing survival items. The threaded butt cap contains a small compass internally and an O-ring for watertightness. The butt cap incorporates a skull-crusher pommel, a feature I really like since one can deliver a devastating downward blow after a slash or parry without changing the basic grip on the knife. This feature also works for puncturing cans. The knife's excellent balance, well-designed blade, and skull crusher combine to make the Sly II one of the best fighting knives of the hollow-handled survival breed.

The Sly II's sheath is of top-grade brown cow-hide, but it is also available in black if so desired. It includes a tie-down tab with a rawhide thong so the sheath can be strapped to the thigh. Holes in the frog allow the sheath to be lashed to the webbed gear for military or paramilitary usage. Instead of a sharpening stone, the Sly II incorporates a Model M, EZ Lap diamond sharpener in a pocket on the front of the sheath.

The Sly II is the most expensive hollow-handled survival knife covered in this book, but it is also a very high-quality example of the blade-maker's art. The combination of the Sly II's quality and its use by the film character Rambo explains its high price tag, which is about $600. The Sly II is, in fact, such a handsome knife that one wants to just gaze at it in appreciation, but its rugged, eye-catching design should not cloud the fact that it is also a well-designed tool, albeit an expensive one.

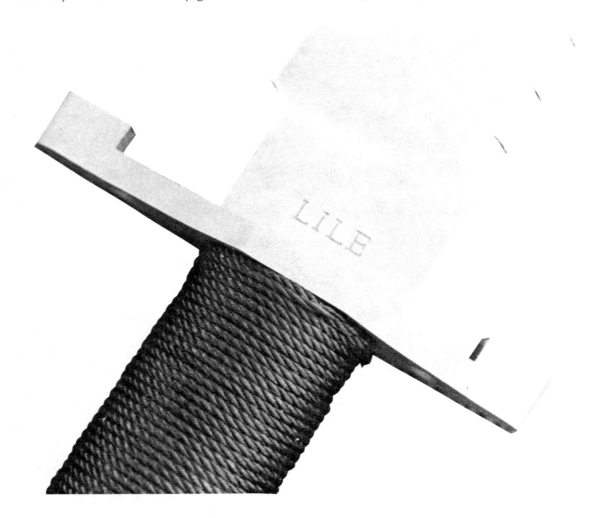

The heavy lugged crossguard on the Sly II can be used for parrying as well as for general-purpose application. Note the "LILE" marking.

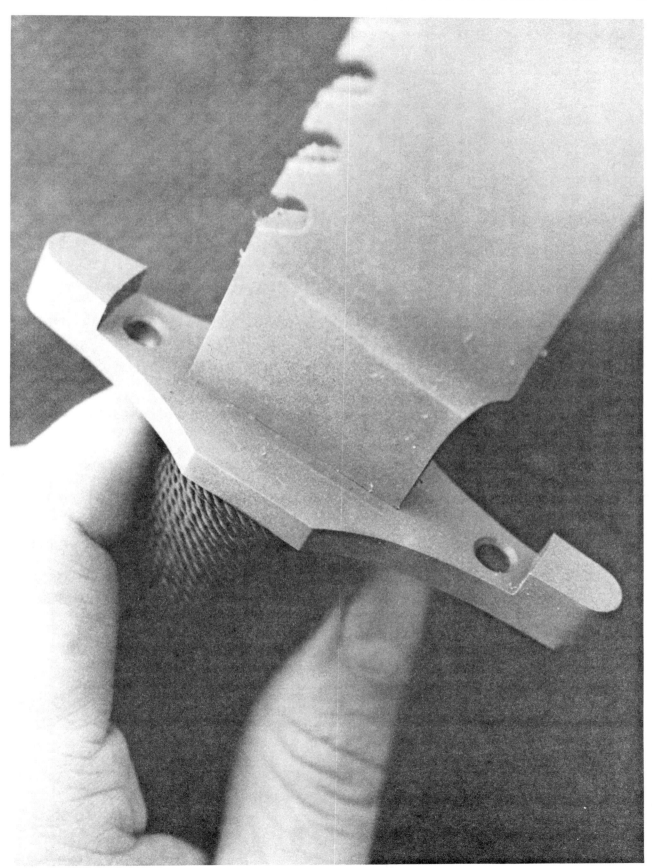

The holes in the crossguard allow the Sly II to be lashed to a shaft when used as a spear point.

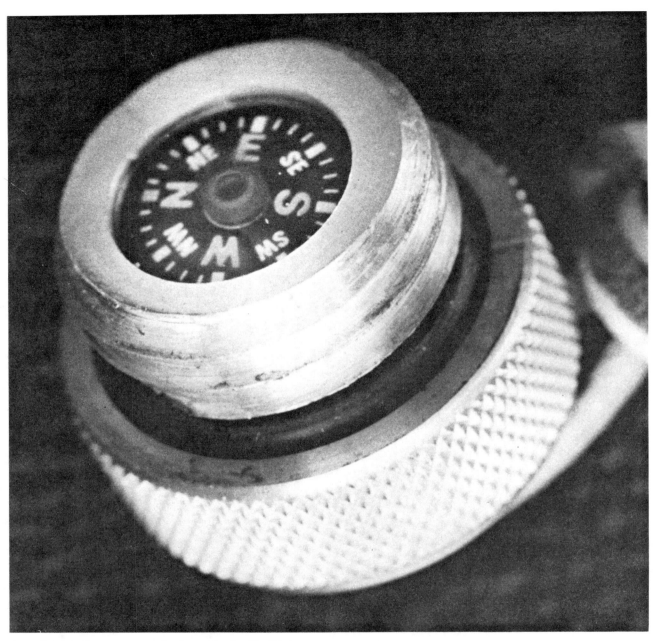

A useful, small compass can be found in the Sly II's butt cap.

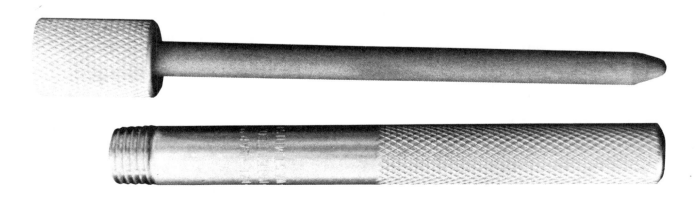

This Model M, E Z Lap sharpener comes with the Sly II.

The Sly II is shown beside the Randall Model 18, the first of the hollow-handled survival knives.

PARRISH SURVIVAL/FIGHTING KNIFE

This large knife from Robert Parrish, also known as the RP, is the one I now use as my standard heavy-duty survival knife. It has also gained wide acceptance with military special operations units, ranging from the French paras to the U.S. Special Forces. Like the Sly II, the Parrish is a big, impressive knife, though its lines are more heavy and functional. It costs only a little over one-third of the Sly II's price tag.

The Parrish has a massive 440-C stainless blade, 8 x 1-1/2 x 1/4 inches, which is heat-treated to Rockwell 57-58. For added strength, the spear point has extra metal at the point most likely to snap when used for prying. The weight of the blade is distributed toward the rear to make it more effective for hacking. Unlike some hollow-handled designs in which one is hesitant to hack or chop with any force out of fear the blade will separate from the handle, the Parrish has an incredibly sturdy system for mating the blade to the handle. The tang is threaded to the handle, with the crossguard in between, and the whole thing is then epoxied. So far, my Parrish has seen heavy use on three continents and under assorted conditions and has "survived" admirably.

Like other knives of the type, the Parrish Survival/Fighting knife has saw teeth along the top of the blade. It should be noted, however, that these are the most effective saw teeth I've ever used. They are the full-width of the blade and arranged in three rows. Though designed only to cut on the draw stroke, these teeth are so effective that one can quickly cut through two- to three-inch limbs without binding. Since conserving energy in a survival situation is important, a saw that does the job with the least effort is very desirable, and the Parrish easily fills the bill.

The heavy crossguard is of 300 series stainless steel, also matte-finished. It has two holes on one side for a wrist thong or the hypothetical lashing for spear usage.

The hollow handle and butt cap are also of 300 series stainless steel and are matte-finished. On a knife which sees a lot of military usage, as does the Parrish, the matte stainless finish is very desirable since it reflects less. Some individuals like to have a small polished area on the blade which can function as a signal mirror, but I leave a matte finish entirely matte. The internal area of the hollow handle, in which you can store survival items, is 2-3/4 inches long and 13/16 inches wide. Although the Parrish does not come with a built-in compass, the company is in the process of developing a spring-mounted compass which will fit inside the butt cap and will not be affected when the butt is used for pounding. An O-ring is used on the butt cap to keep the handle's storage area watertight. I can attest that it works, too, since my knife has taken some dunkings, and the contents of the handle have remained dry.

Parrish offers two sheaths for the RP knife. The standard natural leather one is both sewn and riveted. It has a pocket on the front which holds a sharpening stone. This sheath is designed to be worn either on the belt or lashed to the webbed gear.

The other sheath, which is the one I use, should be of special interest to anyone involved in military "special ops." It costs more, but it's very useful. This "Combat Jump Scabbard" is of black Cordura nylon and has a belt loop that is adjustable for length of drop. It also has two nylon leg straps so that it can be strapped down. The safety strap and flap for the sharpening-stone pocket both use Velcro closures. The knife therefore cannot penetrate the scabbard, the interior of which is lined with Lexan. Though it's not as pretty as some leather sheaths, this sheath really works and keeps the knife exactly where one wants it along the thigh.

I obviously think very highly of the RP Survival/Fighter or I wouldn't have chosen one as the knife that goes with me to far-off places. The Parrish is a no-nonsense, general-purpose survival knife which can also slit a throat or otherwise discommode an enemy if necessary. It is designed for the military special-ops trooper who really uses his knife extensively.

RANDALL MODEL 18, ATTACK/SURVIVAL KNIFE

I acquired my first Model 18 over seventeen years ago in the Republic of Vietnam from a buddy who wanted my Model 60 S&W badly enough to offer a lot more than it was worth, including the Model 18. The Model 18 wasn't

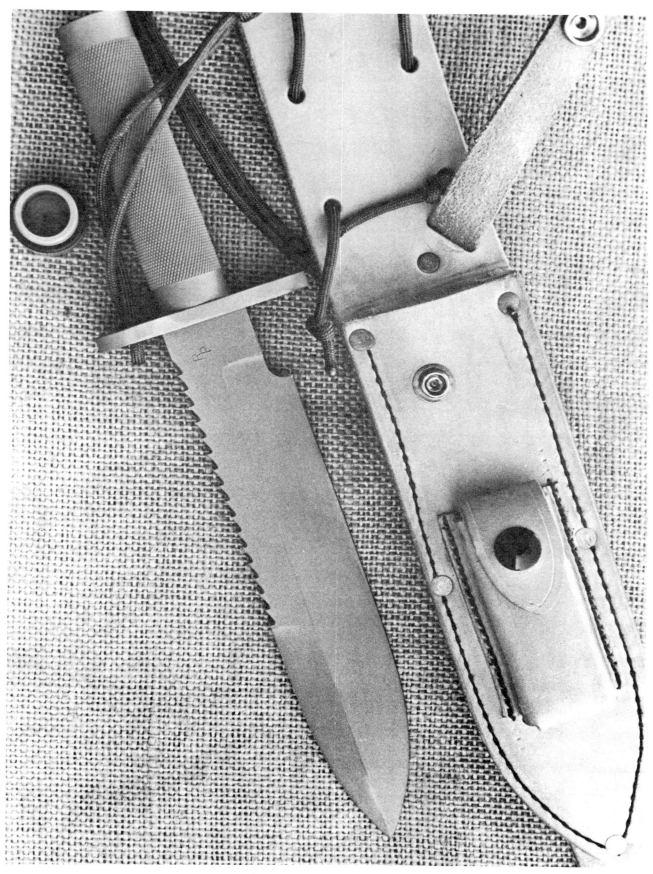

The leather sheath comes standard with the RP Custom Fighting and Survival Knife, which has a heavy spear point and very effective saw teeth.

The wrist thong on the RP prevents the knife user from losing the knife should it be dropped.

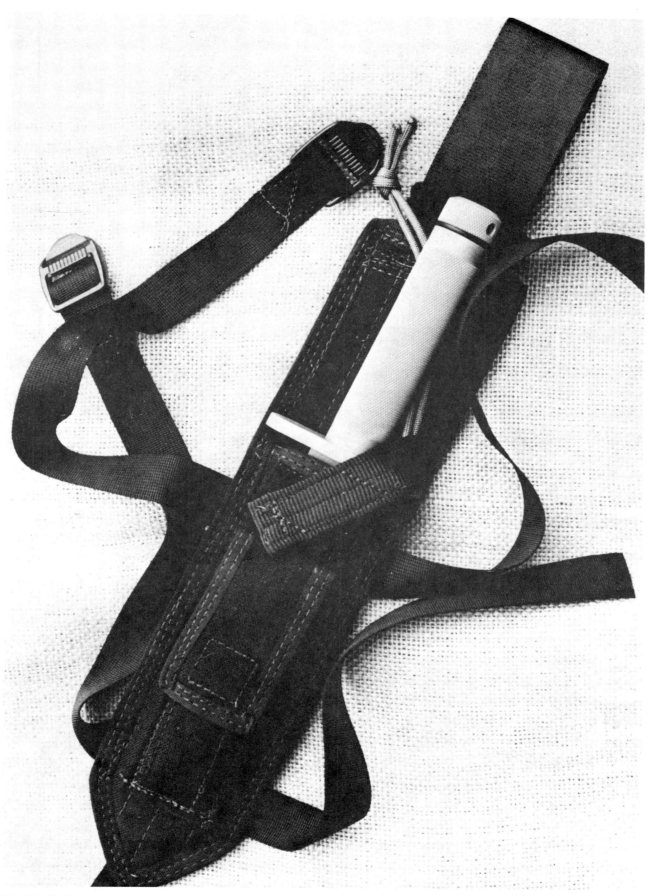

The RP Knife is shown in the Combat Jump Scabbard, which is very useful to military or SWAT personnel.

The Randall Model 18 with its 5-1/2-inch blade appears here beside another symbol of quality, a Rolex watch. Note the "S" on the blade which identifies it as stainless steel.

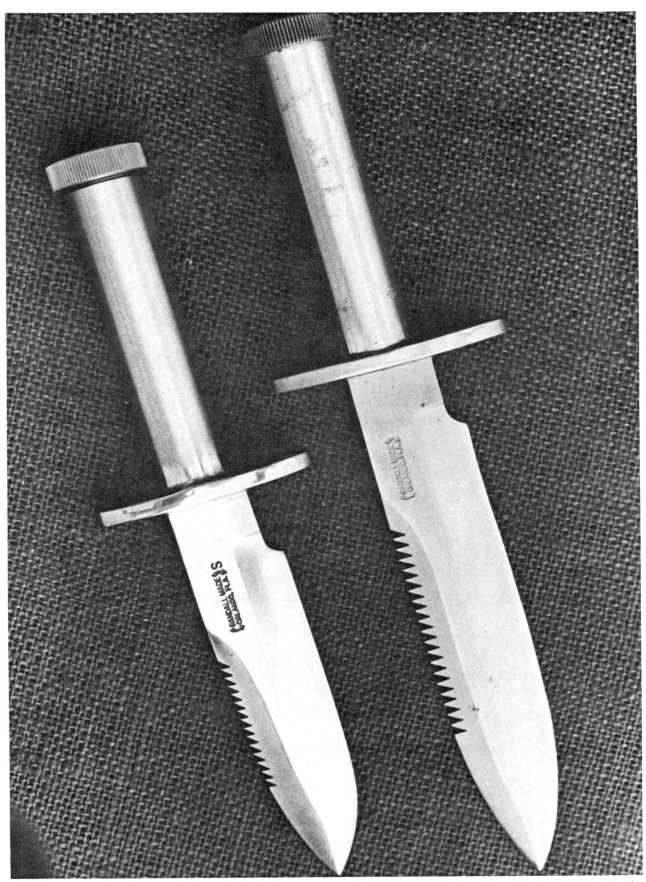

The Randall Model 18 with a 5-1/2-inch blade is shown next to the Model 18 with a 7-1/2-inch blade, which has had its blade sandblasted.

the first hollow-handled survival knife, but for many years it was probably the most widely used. I have owned four Model 18s during the last two decades and still have two of them. I have probably used the Model 18 in the field more than any other knife I own, except perhaps for my Swiss Army Knife. I can honestly say that the Model 18 has always performed excellent service, but then it's a Randall, isn't it?

The Model 18 has a spear-point blade which is available in lengths of 5-1/2 or 7-1/2 inches, either in stainless steel or high-carbon Swedish steel. Currently, I have 7-1/2-inch tool steel and 5-1/2-inch stainless steel versions. Although the 7-1/2-inch version actually looks more symmetrical and sturdy, I've found the 5-1/2-inch blade to be handier. Both are well-balanced blades which will take and hold an excellent edge. The twenty saw teeth are very sharp and work especially well on heavy fabric, sheet metals, etc. They will also perform adequately on wood, though not as well as the Parrish.

The brass crossguard is silver-soldered between the blade and the crossguard. It has a hole on each side which can be used for a wrist thong or to lash the knife to a pole.

The hollow handle is of stainless steel, sealed with a threaded brass butt cap with an O-ring. The hilt, which is smooth and polished, offers a rather slippery gripping surface. You can wrap the hilt with fish line or snare line, thereby creating a gripping surface, and also carry an additional survival item without taking up space inside the handle.

The Model 18's sheath is Randall's "C" model of oil-tanned saddle leather, which is very heavily stitched. Fitted with a pocket for the sharpening stone, the sheath comes with a tie-down thong. It also has thongs for lacing it to the webbed gear since the Model 18 is geared to the military market.

Randall knives are of excellent quality and hold their value well, which makes them a good investment. The Model 18 is a fine survival knife, which can still double as a fighting blade if needed. I recommend it highly. My only objection to the Model 18, in fact, arises from the fact that it is so sought-after that one will often have to wait years for the knife if it's ordered directly from Randall. There are certain dealers who will have the Model 18 or

other Randalls in stock, but one will often have to pay a premium price to get one immediately. Active-duty military personnel can normally get faster delivery from Randall if they are serving in a "combat zone."

I can recommend the above-mentioned custom hollow-handled survivors based on my experience with them in the field. Any one of them would be an excellent choice, since the special characteristics of each could suit your specific needs. Of the custom hollow-handled survival knives I have examined, but not field-tested, the following appear to be acceptable: Timberline, England, Crain, Baskett, and Cox. Another interesting hollow-handled model is one from Tom Enos, who offers a full tang with a slot beneath the scales for the survival items. This model was made to the design of survival-knife expert J.E. Smith.

VICTOR II SURVIVAL SYSTEM

Before ending this chapter, there is one other blade I want to cover, though in some ways it should be evaluated in the utility knife chapter. Since the knife incorporates a survival kit in its sheath, however, I feel it merits discussion here. The knife I am referring to is the Victor II, which is crafted by A. Daniel Valois.

The Victor II Survival System consists of the knife, its sheath, and the very comprehensive survival kit contained in the sheath. The blade, which is of 440-C stainless steel and hardened to 56-58 Rockwell, is 7 inches long with a 3-inch minor cutting edge on the clip. Unlike the hollow-handled knives, the Victor II has a full-length tang, although it does contain two half-inch-diameter stash areas for storing gold, jewels, or other barter items. The tang is especially designed to take certain tools contained in the survival kit. The wooden grip panels are of layered laminated wood, which form a camouflage pattern.

Sandblasted to create a nonglare finish, this one-pound knife has a brass or aluminum crossguard, depending upon individual choice. Very well-balanced with its weight toward the back of the blade, the knife can be wielded effectively when hacking and also handles well when used for slashing during a knife fight.

The sheath is surprisingly compact, consid-

The Victor II Survival System consists of the knife, a sheath with a pocket for survival items, and the survival kit.

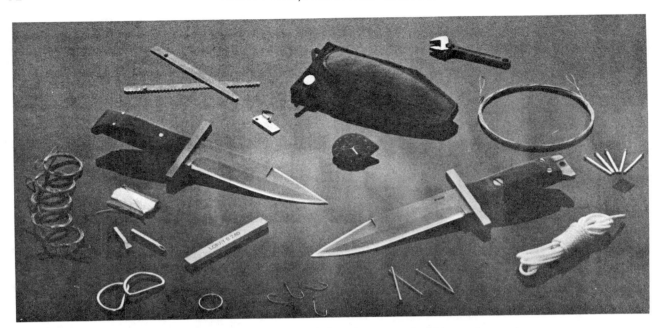

The objects carried in the Victor II Survival System's well-thought-out survival kit are shown above.

ering it contains a comprehensive survival kit in the pouch on the front of the sheath. Fully packed, in fact, it's only one-inch thick. The sheath is of black leather and has a snap retaining strap. Woven through the back of the sheath is a heavy-duty nylon cord which can be used to lash the sheath to one's gear. This system is effective and, though I often lash a sheath to my webbed gear, I'm conditioned to having a belt loop available and would like to see one on the Victor II sheath as well.

The survival kit, which is in the pouch, makes up the remainder of the Victor II Survival System. Included are the following items: twenty-five feet of stainless-steel wire rope with loop cords, five five-foot stainless-steel snare wires, Phillips and blade screwdriver bits that fit into the tang, a liquid-filled Silva compass, one small adjustable wrench (which handles nuts up to half an inch), six feet of nylon 370-pound test rope, two six-inch saw blades (one hacksaw, and one for wood and plastic) which fit into the tang, a Loray sharpening stone, four No. 1 fish hooks, five fireproof and waterproof matches with a waterproof striker, fifty feet of thirty-five-pound test fishing or sewing line, a sewing needle, one P-38 can opener, two D-rings (for making snares and garrotes), one slip ring, and four six-penny nails (useful in making snares and traps).

Obviously, A. Daniel Valois has given a lot of thought to this kit, having chosen very high-quality components. Quality is of supreme importance when one's life may depend on a particular item, and the Victor II Survival System is a quality item. It also offers an excellent compact survival system for those who dislike the hollow-handled knife and want a full-tanged blade. Although I normally carry my Parrish knife on my gun belt for general usage, I think so highly of the Victor II system that if I know I'll be traveling in really rough country or am in other situations where I'm wearing a pack, I generally strap the Victor II onto the frame for added insurance.

If it hasn't already become clear, I'll unequivocally state that I believe the hollow-handled survival knife (or the Victor II system as a substitute) is an invaluable tool for the serious outdoorsman, soldier, game warden, bush pilot, or anyone who might have to keep himself alive with just the items carried on his person. Of course, how well one chooses the survival gear he carries with his knife and how effectively he uses the knife can be even more important than the choice of blade. Use of the knife and choice of survival kit, therefore, will be covered in the next chapter.

5.
Survival Knives and Kits

In order to effectively use one of the hollow-handled survival knives discussed in the preceding chapters, you must understand the limitations and capabilities of your knife and give careful thought to what items will be packed into that limited storage space. The knives that come with a preassembled survival kit may save you such a task, but these kits need to be supplemented in many cases.

When assembling a mini-survival kit to be carried in a survival knife, bear in mind that such a kit is intended for a situation in which more comprehensive kits carried in packs or elsewhere have been lost. In fact, I would normally recommend that the kit contained in the hilt of the knife be one's third reserve. The first-line kit would, of course, be contained in one's pack or stowed away in a safe place within a plane, RV, or boat. A second kit, one you either buy or assemble yourself, should be carried in a pocket or in a pouch on the belt. One of the sardine-can-sized, prepacked kits offered by Survival Aids, Brigade Quartermasters, et al., would serve quite well. (One I especially recommend is available in the United Kingdom from J. Wiseman.) The third and final kit would be the one carried in the handle of one's knife.

FIRE STARTING

Given the limited storage area in the handle of even a large survival knife, one must be very selective about what one includes therein. Since fire is important for warmth, signaling, and cooking food—as well as for water purification—some method for providing fire is a must. Lifeboat matches are frequently chosen because of their resistance to wind and dampness, but they work best with a special striking surface, which may need to be glued to one's sheath for ready availability. If you have a sharpening stone with the knife, you may want to determine whether lifeboat matches will work on it. A candle and some type of tinder are useful tools to carry for fire-building. Any candle other than a small birthday candle would, obviously, not fit inside the handle of the knife, however. Tinder in the form of cotton or some other substance might be stuffed in somewhere, but natural tinder is usually available. If not, you can use lint or something in your pockets to serve as tinder. Due to the fact that one can improvise with tinder materials, I normally would not waste room in my knife's hilt for tinder. One fire-starting aid I do try to include, though, is a compact flint just in case I run out of matches. Because most survival flints or magnesium fire-starters come equipped with a key chain, I affix either one to the back of my sheath with the chain and then wrap a few feet of line around it and the sheath to keep the fire-starter from moving around.

LINE

Speaking of line, you should include a substantial amount of nylon fishing line for use in fishing, sewing, tying together branches for shelter, building traps, and assorted other uses. Stainless-steel wire with a tensile strength of over one hundred pounds is also useful for building shelters and making snares. Although a reasonable amount of line and wire can be placed inside the handle of a survival knife, the most efficient way to do so is to wrap the knife's handle with them. I normally wrap a bottom layer of snare line around a top layer of nylon line. On my Parrish survival knife, I can usually get forty to fifty feet of wire and more than fifty feet of nylon line on if I wrap them tightly, yet I have only one layer of each material. The nylon line normally makes a surprisingly good gripping surface, though some knife owners like to cover the whole thing with tape.

NEEDLES

A needle should be included since it can be used to repair clothing, sew wounds, remove splinters, and create a makeshift compass. To use a needle as a compass, stroke it with a piece of silk in one direction (normally toward the point) and then rub the needle with oil (running a finger over the nose and forehead will normally accumulate a sufficient quantity of oil). With a thread or line, make two loops and carefully lower the needle into a nonmetallic container of still water. Floating by surface tension, the needle should rotate until the head points north (assuming it was stroked from head to point). Even without the rather complicated process of using a needle as a compass, though, a needle doesn't take up much space and is a very useful implement.

COMPASSES

I prefer survival knives that have a compass incorporated inside the butt cap. Once again, I don't consider such a compass to be my primary one, and I normally carry my Prismatik on my belt. Still, it's nice to have a compass in the knife as a backup.

In North America, a watch can be used to create a relatively accurate compass. Be sure the watch is set correctly to the local standard Greenwich time. Lay the watch down faceup with the hour hand pointing directly at the sun. To check this alignment, place a thin stick upright to determine whether its shadow falls along the hour hand. Once the hour hand is aligned with the sun, south will lie midway between the smaller arc between the hour hand and twelve o'clock.

FISHING

Since fishing will often be one of your primary means of obtaining food, a standard item for inclusion is the fish hook. I normally include at least four hooks (to allow for loss) of at least two sizes and three to four small lead sinkers. In addition to fishing, the fish hooks can also be used to make traps for small birds. Although not used strictly for fishing, some small eye screws can be used to build static set fishing lines and snares.

Since fish hooks are invaluable, it's a good idea to use wire between the hook and fishing line to help prevent the line from being bitten in two. Using feathers or bits of cloth, you can also create lures. Another point to remember is that it may be easier to net fish, and if possible one should know how to make a gill net.

HEALTH-CARE ITEMS

Water-purification tablets, Band-Aids, aspirin, and other health-care aids are obviously very important survival items, but, once again, you must consider the amount of room provided in the knife's handle. I have, however, found that a couple of Band-Aids and a couple of butterfly bandages will often fit in the pocket with the sharpening stone on knives having such a pocket. Water-purification tablets don't take up much room and are useful should you need to build a fire to sterilize water. Even more useful, though, is potassium permanganate, commonly found in survival kits used by the Special Air Service. This substance can be used for fire-starting, signaling, water purification, and as an antiseptic. The key is to find a method of packing the potassium permanganate so that it will fit in the handle of one's knife.

ADDITIONAL ITEMS TO BE CARRIED

Two other items I try to store with my survival knife if I'm likely to be in the desert—a possibility I must consider since I sometimes work in the Middle East—are about six feet of quarter-inch plastic tubing and about six square feet of thin clear plastic. Useful in making a solar still, these items will not fit in the handle of a knife and must therefore be lashed to the sheath. My sheath sometimes ends up with a few extra things wrapped around it, but the added items rarely add enough bulk to cause problems, and their additional weight is negligible.

THE "MAP" POCKET

I'd like to see more manufacturers, in fact, offer a second pocket on the back of the sheath, perhaps even one made of thin nylon which would function much as a car's "map pocket." Such items as a map of one's area of operation and solar-still plastic can be carried in such a pocket. A bulky pocket on the rear of the sheath would most likely get in the way or rub the thigh, but such a pocket for flat items shouldn't cause problems.

KNIFE TIPS

Once you have chosen a good survival knife and stocked its hollow handle with the proper items, be sure to employ the knife properly. The knife is a great tool but only if it is used intelligently and skillfully.

Don't abuse the knife, which is your primary survival tool. Since the idea of tying my principal tool on the end of a shaft and possibly losing it while employing it as a harpoon or spear is one I find especially distasteful, I normally don't recommend using a knife for a spear. In wild-pig country, maybe, but normally I advise against it. For fishing, especially, such spears are normally not as effective as a gill net anyway.

Even with a very durable spear-pointed blade, one must be careful of using the knife as a crow-bar. Even high-quality stainless-steel knives will break if enough pressure is applied. Likewise, don't abuse the saw teeth along a knife's top edge: even the most efficient survival-knife saw teeth aren't intended to cut up an engine block or saw down a redwood tree.

Bear in mind the limitations of a knife's cutting edge. A heavy, general-purpose survival knife that is well suited for use as a small hatchet is not likely to handle like a surgical instrument when one has to dress small game. The best compromise is to carry a folding knife as a companion to one's large hollow-handled survivor. My personal choice is a Swiss Army Knife, which may not be a perfect skinning or filleting knife, but it is easier to handle than a larger knife and offers great versatility.

The author is not concerned that the Randall Model 18's blade will separate from the hilt as he applies 195 pounds of weight behind his hacking strokes.

The best saw by far on any knife tested for this book is that found on the Parrish combat/survival knife. In only a few strokes, it easily cut almost completely through this thick branch.

Though the Parrish is a large, heavy knife, it can still be used effectively for shaving tinder.

When using a large blade as found on a heavy survival knife to skin or gut game, take special care not to cut so deeply that the gall or urine bladder is punctured. (Such a puncture would taint the meat.) If the edge near the point of the survival knife is kept very sharp, it can certainly be used effectively in preparing meat when a smaller blade is not available.

A friend of mine from the Special Air Service, an expert on survival, believes that it is important to have different parts of the knife's cutting edge sharpened to different degrees for different uses. I concur with his viewpoint to the extent that I like the first two or three inches to be razor sharp, while further back toward the hilt I prefer a more axe-like cutting edge for hacking. Since a survival knife will be used a great deal for hacking and sharpening poles for building shelter, fish traps, and animal traps, knife sharpness is an important consideration.

Having a very sharp portion on a blade is useful for creating the tinder, such as wood shavings or bark, needed to build a fire. Sawdust left from using the knife's saw blade can make excellent tinder. Bird down, dry straw, and various other natural materials also make good tinder.

A knife's balance and usefulness as a slash-and-thrust weapon must also be considered. The possibility of using a knife to silently eliminate a human enemy exists primarily for the soldier carrying a survival/fighting knife. Quite often, however, the design of a general-purpose knife does not lend itself well to the carotid thrust or the other more rapid killing techniques.

Probably the easiest way to make my basic point about the hollow-handled survival knife is to re-emphasize the fact that it is by its nature a compromise between size and convenience, and it is designed to perform a large number of tasks adequately rather than one or two in an outstanding fashion. Likewise, one cannot expect to pack a *comprehensive* survival kit into the space available in the handle of the knife, but a survival kit should be available in a knife's handle should you need one as a final resort.

Because of the limitations of the hollow-handled survival knife, I recommend that it be supplemented with a good pocket knife such as a Swiss Army Knife, accurate compass, map, firearm, and a more-comprehensive, pocket survival kit. All these items can be easily carried on the belt or in the pockets, thereby ensuring their propinquity if needed. When choosing a hollow-handled survival knife for everyday use, I highly recommend you choose either a high-quality, custom knife (such as the Parrish or Randall) or the best of the production knives (such as the Brewer Explorer) so that it can hold up under heavy usage. If one is picking a survival kit to store at a "retreat" or in one's home, the highest-quality knife possible should also be chosen, though some of the prepackaged inexpensive kits (such as those from Lifeknife) are useful since they can be purchased in multiples and stored in vehicles, boats, and planes.

One of the most basic rules of survival is that you keep your head and this applies to the acquisition of food and shelter, navigation, signaling to extract oneself, and the use of one's knife. The survival knife will be your second most basic tool—your mind will be your first.

6.
Folding General-Purpose and Survival Knives

Beyond a doubt, the handiest knives discussed in this work are those "folders" which fit into a pocket or a pouch on the belt. In addition to being handy, such knives can be used for a myriad of tasks where a certain delicacy of touch may be required (such as skinning). The folder also has the great advantage of propinquity; one can easily have it along most of the time.

CHOOSING A FOLDER

Buck and Gerber, among others, offer quite durable and effective production folders which will suffice for most tasks. The main point to remember in choosing a folder is not to buy one that is too large, or you could otherwise carry a sheath knife just as easily! Be sure that any knife intended for medium or heavy usage has a locking blade.

SERE/ATTACK KNIFE

There are many good custom-made folders on the market, and you can follow your own preference in choosing the one that has the right feel. A good representative example is the "SERE/Attack" designed by Al Mar with the Special Forces trooper in mind. (SERE stands for Survival, Escape, Resistance, Evasion.) When open, this sturdy and well-balanced folder has an overall length of 10-1/2 inches, 4-1/2 inches of which is blade. The blade locks open as any good utility folder should. The scales for the knife are of camo green Micarta. This knife is designed primarily for utility/survival usage, though in a pinch it can also serve as a viable fighting knife. The SERE comes with a leather scabbard in either black or woodland camo pattern.

SWISS ARMY KNIFE

By far the most useful folding knife remains the Swiss Army Knife. Beware of the tendency, however, to choose a knife loaded with tools that is then too large to fit into a pocket. Also beware of choosing cheap imitations. It's far better to pay a little more for a Victorinox.

For survival/general-purpose usage, there are four types of Swiss Army Knives by Victorinox worthy of consideration: the Champion, Pioneer, Huntsman, and Tinker.

Champion

The Champion is the largest of these four, which hampers its portability a bit; however, the fact that it includes so many blades and implements makes it a good knife to tuck into a large pocket when outdoors. It's also an especially good one to use to illustrate the versatility of the Swiss Army Knife genre by discussing the Champion's tools and their various applications:

- *Large blade.* At 2-1/2 inches, this blade will do most of the utility cutting one expects from a small folding knife. I use it primarily for cutting twine or apples or for some other mundane chores, but in a pinch it could be used for skinning and cleaning small game. I have also used it for shaving off dried bark for use as tinder.
- *Small blade.* The smaller blade is only 1-1/2 inches in overall length and is a useful supplement to the larger blade for cutting tasks. Both this blade as well as the larger one take an edge well and hold it through a lot of use if one shows reasonable judgment.
- *Corkscrew.* Only someone who has found

The Al Mar **SERE/ATTACK** is an outstanding folding fighting/utility knife. It is much larger and more durable than can be shown in this photo and I highly recommend it.

A Victorinox Champion is displayed with its various tools and blades.

The Swiss Army Knife's saw blade will really cut wood; it is, in fact, one of the most effective saws on a knife I have ever used.

One use for the Swiss Army Knife is to shave bark for use as tinder.

himself with a bottle of wine and no cork-screw can understand how useful this implement is. I have also used the corkscrew once or twice as a makeshift drill in light wood, though I don't normally recommend the practice; in an emergency, though, it will do the job.

- *Can opener.* The can opener on the Swiss Army Knife actually works quite well. Over the years, I've opened at least fifty cans with this type of can opener, including some fairly heavy-gauge ones. It takes a bit of practice and effort to achieve maximum proficiency with this little can opener, but it does work reliably.

- *Small screwdriver.* On the top of the can-opener blade is a small screwdriver blade. Some of the tasks I've used it for include setting adjustable sights on handguns and tightening screws on my glasses. I've also used it for very light prying jobs where it was necessary to get a thin blade under something in order to open it.

- *Bottle-cap lifter.* In addition to normal metal pry caps, I've also used this device on the plastic type found on brake fluid or gas line deicer.

- *Large screwdriver.* This blade is located on the end of the bottle opener and is useful for larger screws and for some types of prying. Note, however, that you need to be careful that the blade doesn't close on your fingers when torquing a screw with any force.

- *Wire stripper.* Though I rarely use this feature, it's useful and doesn't take up any additional room. It certainly is faster than using the regular knife blade to strip a wire.

- *Reamer.* I usually think of this blade as an awl or leather punch, though it serves a lot of purposes. In many survival situations, the ability to punch a hole in leather can be important. Anyone who has lost pounds while on an extended patrol can attest to the value of being able to take one's belt in. Like the screwdriver blade, this is a very useful tool, but one must make sure it doesn't close on the fingers while in use.

- *Scissors.* I didn't realize until I started carrying my Swiss Army Knife how often

one needs scissors. I would estimate that I've used the scissors on my Victorinoxes more than any other blade. Cutting finger-nails, trimming my mustache, cutting out ads or coupons—the list of more mundane uses is long. In a survival situation, the ability to cut out a jerkin or other rough clothing from a tarpaulin or heavy cloth could be quite useful, and though the scissors on the Swiss Army Knife certainly aren't heavy-duty shears, they are nevertheless surprisingly handy and durable. Other uses include cutting leather thongs for traps or snares, cutting signal panels from cloth or other material, or cutting strips of cloth.

- *Phillips screwdriver.* I've found this blade invaluable for mechanical and minor car repairs. Phillips screwdrivers are often hard to find when one needs them, and it's a real boon to always have one along. It takes a bit of practice with the Swiss Army Knife to keep the constant pressure on the Phillips head so it doesn't slip out, but it does work.

- *Magnifying glass.* I really did use this device on my Champion a couple of times to read fine print. In a survival situation, the glass can theoretically be used for starting fires, and I have managed to do so. One must, however, have patience, good tinder, and strong sunlight to focus.

- *Wood saw.* Never underestimate the wood saw on a Victorinox. The one on my Champion is extremely effective on limbs up to 1-1/2 inches in diameter and can saw through them with great speed. This saw cuts on both the forward and backward strokes, which can therefore enhance its efficiency.

- *Fish scaler.* Whether in a survival situation or on a fishing trip, this device can be quite useful. I've only used the one on my Victorinox once, but it worked adequately.

- *Hook disgorger.* Located on the end of the scaler blade, this is one of those features which takes up no extra room but is exceptionally useful and saves a lot of wear and tear on the fingers—a consideration for survival when infection could be a problem.

- *Ruler.* Incorporated into the scaler blade,

Although it is not as easy to start fires with a magnifying lens as some adventure novels would lead one to believe, I have managed to do so with patience and very dry tinder.

Some of the Champion's features are highlighted here: file/metal saw, fish scaler/hook disgorger/ruler and wood saw blades.

the ruler is in both centimeters and inches and can be used to measure objects up to about three inches in diameter or length. I've used mine a few times in hardware stores when buying bolts or other parts.

- *Metal file.* Intended for use on the nails, this file in a pinch can, along with the hacksaw edge, convert a piece of thin sheet metal into an arrowhead, fishing spearpoint, or other implement.
- *Hacksaw.* The edge of the file blade is a light-duty hacksaw. I've only used this saw once to cut through a quarter-inch screw, but it did the job reasonably effectively. It could serve in a complete survival situation to rough-cut an arrowhead or other implement from sheet metal.
- *Fine screwdriver.* My Champion includes a fine screwdriver blade in addition to the fine screwdriver on the can-opener blade. I don't really know the reason for having two such blades, though the separate blade should be more effective on a tighter screw since it allows more leverage.
- *Tweezers.* I have found the tweezers which tuck into the grip of the Swiss Army Knife to be among its most useful features. Their usefulness in removing splinters is, of course, a boon, but I have also retrieved more than one small object from a crack or crevice with them.
- *Toothpick.* The toothpick, which tucks into the grip opposite the tweezers, has also proven most useful.

Other Swiss Army Knife Models

The other three Swiss Army Knives incorporate fewer blades, but they are easier to carry in a normal pocket. The Pioneer has a large 2-1/4-inch blade, a large screwdriver, bottle opener, wire stripper, small screwdriver, can opener, and reamer. The Huntsman has a 2-1/4-inch blade, 1-5/8-inch blade, a large screwdriver, bottle opener, wire stripper, small screwdriver, can opener, corkscrew, large scissors, wood saw, reamer, tweezers, and toothpick. The Tinker has a 2-1/4-inch blade, a 1-5/8-inch blade, a large screwdriver, bottle opener, wire stripper, small screwdriver, Phillips screwdriver, can opener, and reamer.

SWISS ARMY KNIFE VARIATIONS

Similar types of knives, known as "Spanish Military Pocket Knives," offer variations of the Swiss Army Knives, some of which include a fork, cartridge hook, or other tools. There is also a West German Army knife which is quite compact and has a cutting blade, saw, screwdriver, bottle opener, corkscrew, and reamer.

In evaluating the Swiss Army type of knife, it is important to bear in mind that in many situations, your "survival" (or at least comfort) may depend on your being able to make a minor car repair with a screwdriver or opening a bottle or can of stew. Therefore, the fact that the Swiss Army Knife's primary blade is not as effective at most tasks as the larger, more sturdy lockable blades on folders such as the Al Mar must be weighed against the versatility of the Swiss Army Knife.

ACE-PAL-O UNIVERSAL SURVIVAL KNIFE

Although it could have been discussed along with the hollow-handled survival knives, the ACE-PAL-O Universal Survival Knife also fits within the context of this chapter since it is that odd hybrid, a "hollow-handled" folder. This interesting knife comes with two 3-5/8-inch blades which are interchangeable, the spare fitting into a small pocket inside the pouch. One of the stainless blades has a cutting edge, while the other has a cutting edge with a saw along the top. The blades are easily interchangeable and lock into position using a locking stud. When folded, a slight portion of the blade's base protrudes, thereby functioning as a screwdriver.

Beneath the one clear plastic scale are indentations in the knife's body, in which are stored or affixed certain survival items. Permanently mounted beneath the scales are a small compass and a thermometer. The compass is in actuality a button compass and is not liquid-filled. Personally, I wouldn't have included the thermometer, but it's there.

Within the small indentations are the following loose survival items: a small candle to aid in fire-starting, a fishing kit (line, weight, fly, hook), matches, and small nails.

Mounted on the opposite side of the knife's

handle from the storage section is a small sharpening stone. To use the stone, the blade must first be dismounted. As an additional aid to versatility, the locking stud can be used as a bottle opener. The belt pouch/sheath is of leather and fastens with a large button hole, fitting over the locking stud. A cutout at the base of the sheath allows you to view the compass while the knife is in the sheath.

The ACE-PAL-O is not a particularly high-quality knife, but it is an interesting concept and it is very inexpensive. Like the Lifeknife, it offers good value for storing in places where it might be needed in an emergency, especially since it takes up less room than the Lifeknife.

The number of folders which could be discussed is large, but most comments would quickly become redundant since there aren't that many possible variations. My own recommendation for a folder is the Swiss Army Knife because it is useful for so many tasks. As a result, the Swiss Army Knife or another folder should normally be carried as an adjunct to a belt survival or fighting knife.

The ACE-PAL-O folding/hollow-handled survival knife is shown with its blade open and a survival kit that is visible through the clear scale.

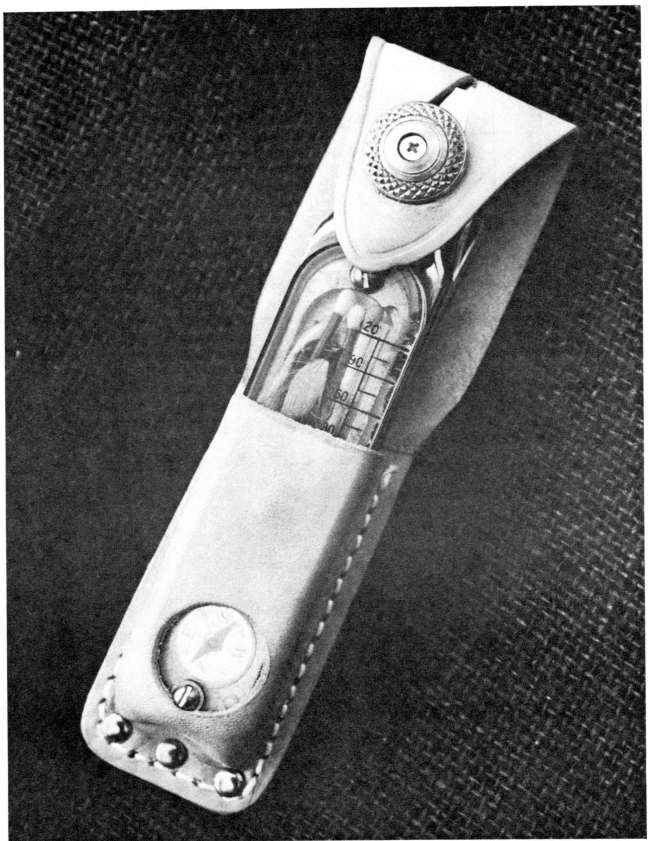

The **ACE-PAL-O** is shown in its sheath. The compass can be viewed through the hole so that the knife user does not have to remove his knife.

7.
Fighting Knives

Virtually any knife can be used as a fighting knife when necessary. My days as a police officer helped convince me that people can do each other in with all sorts of objects should they so desire—and certain knives perform that function better than others. Although I love the lines of the classic fighting dagger, I personally prefer a good Randall or Parrish multipurpose knife. Both Randall's Attack/Survival (Model 18) and Parrish's Survival/Fighting Knife are intended to serve both in and out of combat and do so well. Randall's big Bowie-styles and Lile's Sly II also function well in the fighting/utility role, as does Al Mar's SERE/Attack folder.

Still, the fighting task is secondary, albeit important, for these blades. There are, however, a substantial number of knives designed to be used in close combat with utility application being secondary. The fighting knife is usually designed for delivering thrusts to the brachial, radial, carotid, or subclavian arteries; heart; stomach, or other vital organs; or to slash at the hands, arms, face, or other exposed targets.

Traditionally, fighting knives are of dagger or stiletto type and are designed for thrusts. The best fighting knife, however, must also have a sharp edge or edges so that it can be used for slashes. Assuming a knife will actually be used in a blade-to-blade encounter—which is not all that likely—the ability to deliver both slashes and thrusts makes the weapon more versatile and harder to defend against. In such theoretical blade-to-blade encounters, a crossguard is also very desirable since it allows one to catch an opponent's blade.

A far more likely use for the fighting knife in a military context is as a silent assassination weapon (assuming, that is, that the victim cooperates and dies quietly), with the carotid subclavian thrust normally the quickest means to killing the enemy.

TRENCH WARFARE AND THE KNIFE

The two World Wars saw the proliferation of fighting knives. In World War I, bitter trench fighting saw the birth of all sorts of "trench knives," including a variety of knives which incorporated brass knuckles. So vicious was the hand-to-hand combat in the trenches that such knives really saw action. The Germans developed a wide variety of trench daggers during the "Great War." Most had blades of about 6 inches with one edge along one side and a half edge along the back of the blade. The most well-known World War I trench knife, though, is probably the American 1918 pattern dagger, which has a 6-3/4-inch double-edged blade, brass knuckles, and a skull-crusher pommel.

In the British trenches, knuckle knives were popular as well, especially those from Robbins of Dudley, which made assorted knuckle knives and push daggers. My personal favorite has a 4-inch blade which extends straight out from the brass knuckles in push-dagger fashion. Though it's a collector's piece, I occasionally carried this little Robbins of Dudley along as a companion while a student in London. Many Robbins of Dudley fighting knives turned up in World War II as well, and probably a few made it to Korea and Malaya, among other places.

FAIRBAIRN-SYKES DAGGER

Fighting knives in World War II abounded, but they were often then used by elite units as a symbol and a silent way to eliminate an

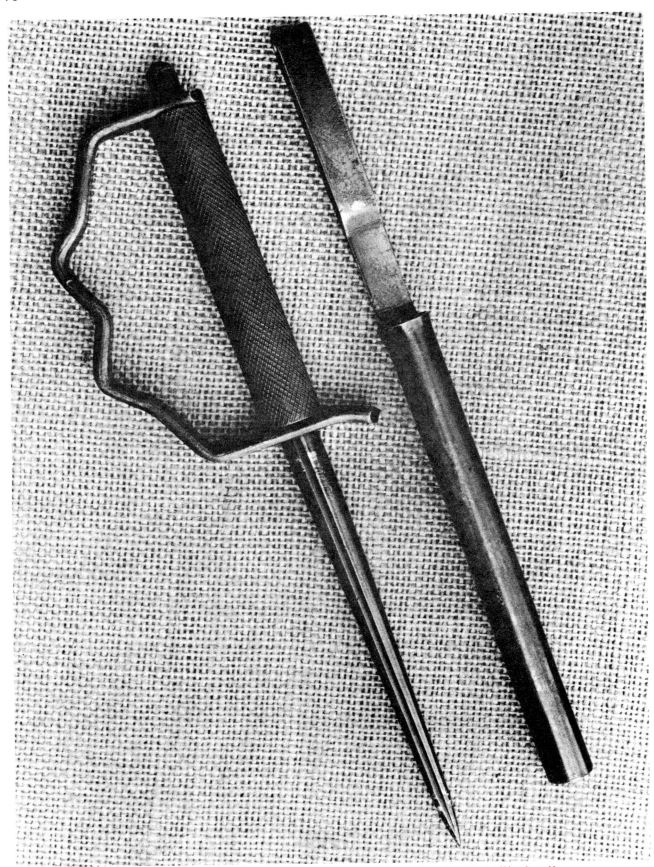

This spike combat knife with a knuckle-duster handguard was probably used during World War I or II.

The Ghurka in the middle of this photo has his kukri ready for action. Photo courtesy of the Imperial War Museum.

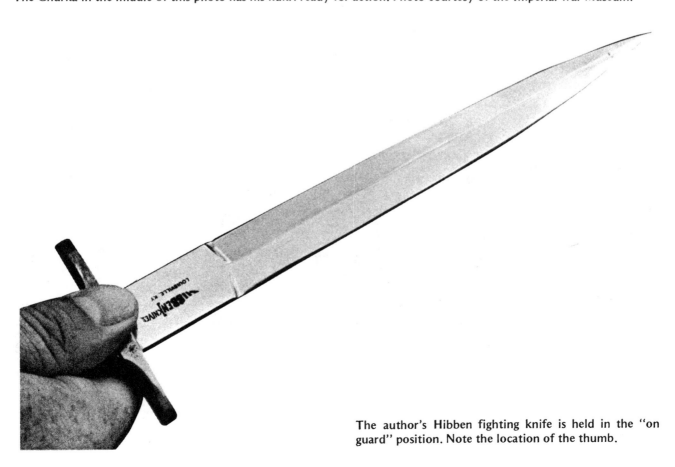

The author's Hibben fighting knife is held in the "on guard" position. Note the location of the thumb.

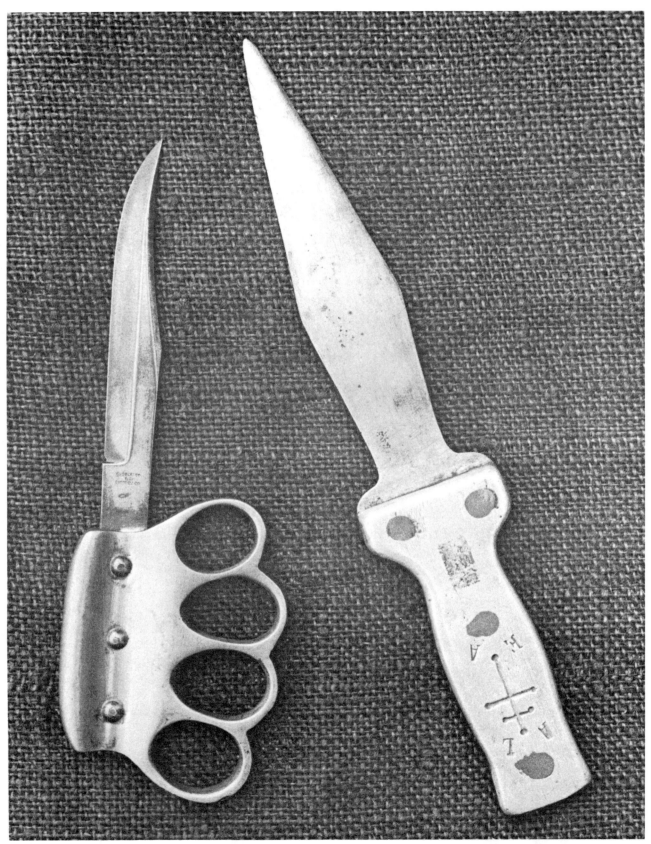

A Robbins of Dudley knuckle knife is shown at left, and a fighting knife made for the French Resistance in World War II appears at right. The placement of the R-D's blade allows easy use when drawing across a throat.

This **Robbins** of **Dudley** knuckle-duster push dagger, used by the British in both World Wars, is obviously a pure fighting blade.

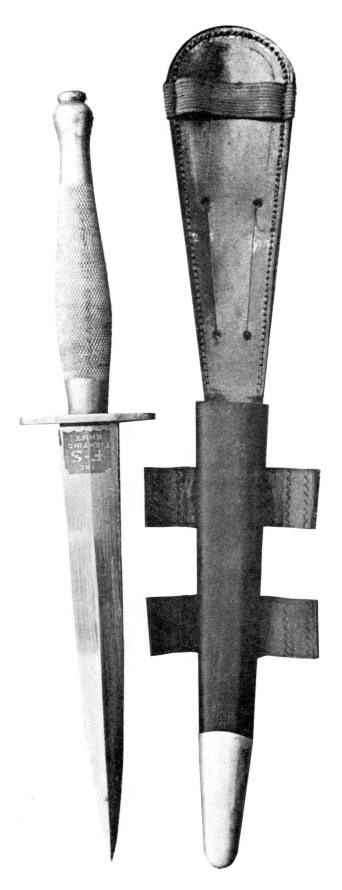

The Fairbairn-Sykes Commando Dagger—the classic fighting knife of all time.

enemy. The most famous fighting knife of all time—the Fairbairn-Sykes (F-S) dagger—was, in fact, designed for use by the British Commandos during their harassment raids against the Germans. With its 6-7/8-inch, double-edged blade and well-known Coke-bottle hilt, the F-S has not only become the archetypal fighting knife, but it is also the symbol of elite units the world over. The F-S proved popular with other troops as well and adequately served its purpose of dealing deadly thrusts to certain arteries or vital organs. As the F-S saw increased usage, however, its faults became apparent: it had a tendency to break off at the point; it tended to roll in the hand because of the hilt's design; and it was not too effective for slashes. These faults were corrected in the Applegate-Fairbairn knife, designed by close-combat experts W.E. Fairbairn and Rex Applegate, and was the successor to the F-S.

V-42 KNIFE

Other F-S-style knives were adopted by American military units. The Office of Strategic Services, Marine Raiders, and 1st Special Service Force all had F-S-type knives, though the V-42 stiletto of the 1st Special Service Force was quite distinctive. The most interesting aspect of the V-42 is the "thumb print" on the ricasso which is supposedly there to remind the user where to place his thumb for proper use of the blade. This design still retains its appeal for many knife makers, and there have been modern copies. In fact, I have a beautifully made Hibben custom fighting knife of V-42 style.

SPECIAL UNIT BLADES OF WORLD WAR II

The Commandos also made use of other specialized fighting knives during World War II. The Smatchett, for example, was a heavy hacking weapon with a 10-1/4-inch leaf-shaped blade. When used with skill, the Smatchett could cleave through a neck or limb with one blow. Another interesting Commando knife was what is known as the "Middle East Commando Knife" because it was fabricated for Commandos serving in the Middle East.

British clandestine units such as the Special Operations Executive had various knives designed for their needs as well. Small concealable

The skull-crusher pommel on this custom Gil Hibben fighting knife, which is based on the V-42 stiletto used by the 1st Special Service Force during World War II, allows the knife to be used to deliver a downward thrust with the back of the hand.

World War II paratrooper's gear includes an array of edged weapons. At left is a machete; behind the .45 is a knuckle-duster fighting knife, and a parachutist's switchblade is shown at bottom right. (It can be used with ease in one hand to cut tangled lines.) Photo courtesy of the U.S. Army.

daggers which could be worn on the arm or beneath a lapel, for example, were developed for agents, while a gravity knife with a secondary spike blade was developed for use by agents and Commandos. The spike blade was found to be very effective for delivering thrusts to the arteries. Also using the spike blade was the McLacklin-Peskett Close Combat Weapon, which ingeniously combined a cosh, spike dagger, and garrote in one weapon.

M3 TRENCH KNIFE

The two most widely used U.S. combat knives during World War II were the Ka-Bar (previously discussed) and the M3 Trench Knife. Developed in 1943, more than 2.5 million M3s were procured during World War II. Like the Ka-Bar, the M3 uses a stacked leather washer handle, which is quite comfortable to grip. Its blade is 6-1/2 inches long with the back edge sharpened about half way back. The butt is of

steel and is pinned in place. On most M3s, one ear of the crossguard is bent while the other is straight. In a theoretical blade-to-blade encounter, the bent ear might work more effectively as a blade catcher or for parrying. Numerous cutlers produced the M3, including Camillus, Case, Imperial Knife Company, PAL, Kinfolks, and Utica. Though it was not the best fighting knife ever developed, the M3 was quite good for a mass-production item.

OTHER AMERICAN WORLD WAR II BLADES

The M4 bayonet for the M1 Carbine, which appears to be quite similar to the M3 Trench Knife, also saw substantial use as a fighting knife. The M5 bayonet for the M1 Garand even saw limited use as a fighting knife.

Various custom knives were used in World War II, including the Randall #1 and the John Ek Commando.

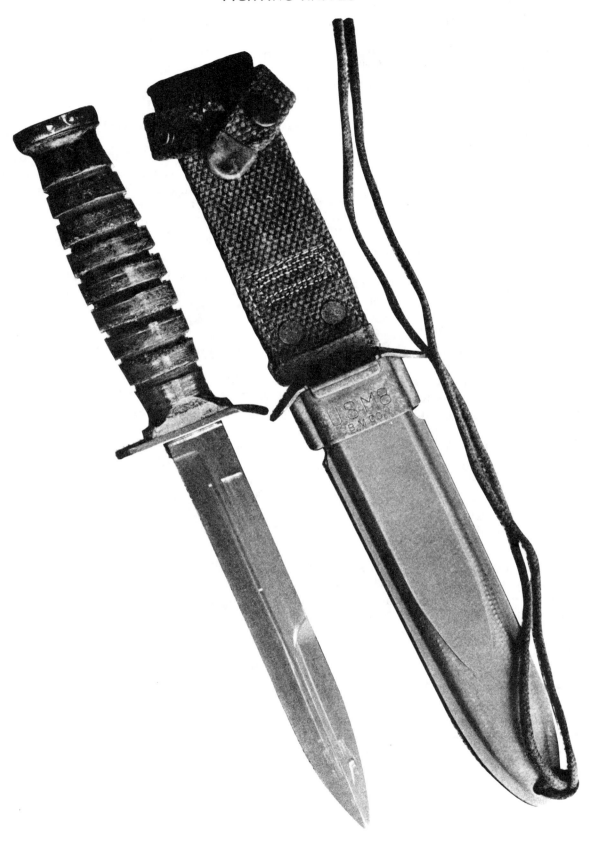

The U.S. Mark 3 Combat Knife was one of the most widely used fighting knives of World War II.

KOREA

During the Korean War, many of the same knives were used, often because World War II vets were recalled and took their trusty blades back into combat with them. The Randall Model 14, which was so popular in Vietnam, first saw combat in Korea.

VIETNAM

During the Vietnam War, the Ka-Bar continued to be issued to the Marines, while other utility/fighting knives (such as the Jet Pilot's Knife) were also issued. There were few pure fighting knives issued in Vietnam, however. Even the "SOG Knife," made on Okinawa for special operations units, was a Bowie-style utility knife.

Gerber Mark II

Among private-purchase fighting knives used in Vietnam, the Gerber Mark II is still one of the best. The Mark II was introduced in 1967, and early models had a slightly offset blade, supposedly to allow a more comfortable wrist position with the "fencing foil" grip and also to hug the body better when carried. More common, however, was the double-edged, compound-curve blade which was not offset. A section of saw teeth appeared on each side of the blade. This 7-inch blade was a good design for fighting and a satisfactory one for utility usage. The crossguard has a hook on each side, and the pommel is designed to act as a "judo stick" to increase its combat effectiveness. The Armor-hide grip is very slip-resistant and is well-designed for wielding the knife. The Mark II is still one of my favorite knives, and I recommend it highly. As commercial fighting knives go, it's hard to beat. For those who want a combat blade which can also serve for survival usage, the Mark II is a viable choice, too. It has already been combat-tested, having seen extensive usage by the Special Forces and SEALs, among other military units.

TANTO

Another commercially available fighting knife of which I think highly is the Cold Steel Tanto. Based on the traditional fighting knife of the samurai, the Tanto is traditional in looks but

contemporary in engineering. Its blade is made of 6-inch stainless steel and is very sturdily constructed. One reason, in fact, so many Tantos see utility usage is that they are so tough. I can testify that mine has held up incredibly well even under very hard usage.

The armor-piercing point, combined with a razor-sharp blade, makes the Tanto a vicious close-quarters weapon, though its crossguard does not serve well for parrying, its one disadvantage in close-quarters usage. The Tanto's Pachmayr-style rubber grip makes it easy to hold on to—another real plus. Its balance is also good for close-quarters combat, though it is not a throwing knife and is not balanced for hurling. The Tanto's sheath is quite useful since it allows the knife to be affixed about one's person in various ways.

OTHER COMMERCIAL KNIVES

Other assorted commercial or military fighting knives are available at quite reasonable prices. There is a West German Army trench knife available, in fact, for under $25 from Atlanta Cutlery. This functional knife has a 5-5/8-inch, stainless-steel blade and is a real bargain at the price. Atlanta Cutlery, in fact, has a large selection of inexpensive and interesting imported fighting knives. Another quality blade in their catalog is billed as the "Anti-Terrorist" knife. In reality, however, this knife is more of a utility knife than a fighting blade.

RANDALL FIGHTING KNIVES

Among custom fighting knives, I have a strong preference for Randalls and would normally choose one of Randall's heavy utility/fighting knives, such as the Model 14. Randall's pure fighting knives, however, are also impressive. I have a Model 2 "Fighting Stiletto," for example, which I dearly love. The Model 2 is available with a 6-inch, 7-inch, or 8-inch blade and has a "modified Fairbairn-Sykes" style grip. Though its grip is roughly of F-S Coke-bottle shape, it is really a bit fuller and does not have the F-S's tendency to twist in the hand.

More impressive but less functional than the Model 2 is the Randall Model 13 "Arkansas Toothpick." This 12-inch-bladed monster is a

The Gerber Mark II is shown at left; the Mark I at right.

The Gerber Mark II, shown here strapped to a calf, is one of the more popular and better fighting/survival/utility knives around. The model shown is an older one and has a gray grip.

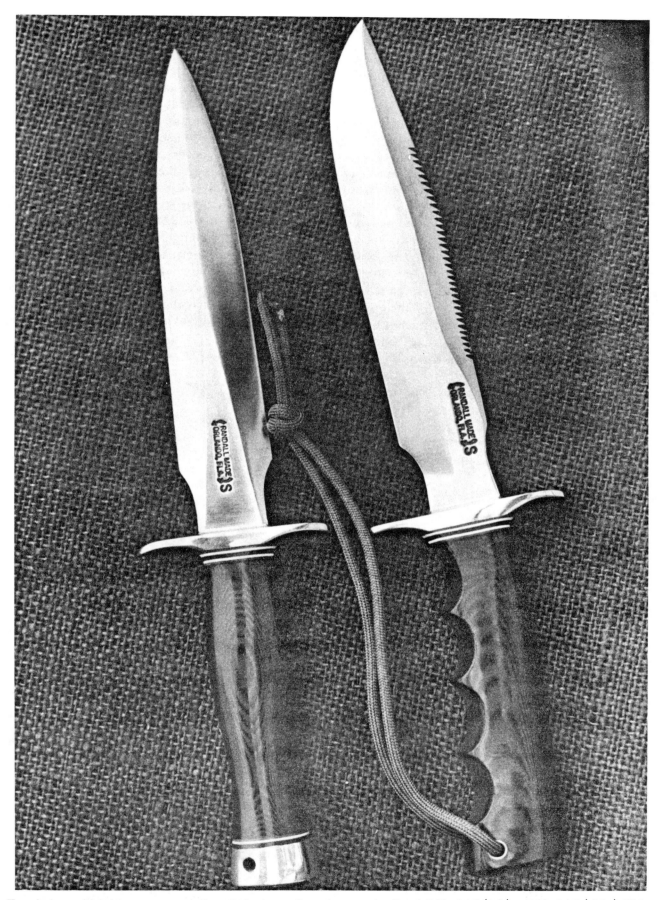

Two knives which have seen more than their share of combat are the Randall Model 2 (left) and Model 1 (right). This Model 1 incorporates saw teeth for more general-purpose use. The Model 2, a stiletto, is intended more for pure combat. The Mark I, used by U.S. military personnel since World War II, is still in substantial use.

replica of the dagger carried by Confederate soldiers in the Civil War, and though a fighting knife, it is rather large by contemporary standards.

APPLEGATE-FAIRBAIRN KNIFE

Another custom fighter I'm especially impressed with is the Applegate-Fairbairn (A-F). Designed by Rex Applegate and W.E. Fairbairn to correct the faults they had discovered in the F-S dagger while training special operations personnel in close combat, the Applegate-Fairbairn is a sturdy, functional fighting knife. Its 6-inch blade is of stainless steel and has a very sturdy profile, especially at the ricasso and the point, which are areas of frequent breakage in the F-S. The A-F takes an excellent edge and is designed to be effective for both slashes and thrusts.

Its crossguard is well-designed for parrying, being of quarter-inch brass hooked forward to catch an enemy's blade.

The A-F's Lexan grip keeps the knife from moving or slipping in the hand, while adjustable weights beneath the grips allow you to adjust the balance to fit your own taste. I should point out, though, that a good fighting knife will normally be hilt-heavy.

CUSTOM KNIFE SELECTION TIPS

There are many other excellent custom fighting knives on the market, and one should use the same rules of thumb I have suggested elsewhere in this work for knife selection. Choose a custom knife that's exactly tailored to your needs and, therefore, can perform tasks better than a production blade. You need to know, of course, what your needs are, however, before choosing a custom blade.

My own taste in fighting knives dictates the following features: a blade of six to eight inches so that the knife can reach out and bite the enemy at a distance. The blade should be such that it can be used for slashes as well as thrusts and parries. As a pure fighting knife, I prefer a stiletto or dagger with a pointed double-edged blade. The crossguard should be designed to allow parries, with a hooked crossguard offering many advantages.

Balance should be good, and should make the knife feel hilt-heavy. The hilt itself should allow a firm grip even if the hands are sweaty or covered with blood, the latter being a distinct possibility in close-combat knife encounters.

Should you choose to use a fighting knife, be sure to train yourself in its use so that any blood that will cover a knife will primarily be that of the enemy rather than your own! Killing sentries stealthily with a knife is no easy matter, and killing an armed enemy who can see you coming is far more difficult. The best knife in the world can't compensate for a clumsy wielder, though the Spetsnaz knife, which shoots its blade at the enemy, can certainly give one the advantage of surprise and distance. By all means, choose a top-notch fighting knife, but do everything you can to make sure your abilities live up to it.

This U.S. Ranger advisor to the Vietnamese Rangers has a Randall Model 2 fighting dagger as his blade. Photo courtesy of the U.S. Army.

The Applegate-Fairbairn fighting knife combines the combat knowledge of two of the twentieth century's foremost knife experts.

8.
Street Survival Knives

Although most of the knives discussed in this book are intended for use on the battlefield or in the wilderness, those covered in this chapter are designed for that highly specialized field of urban combat—escape and evasion on the battlefield of the streets. Many knives intended for such usage, though marginally better than no weapon at all, are virtually useless in a real confrontation. Even those which are relatively effective must be used with some degree of skill. As a result, you must not only choose a "street combat" blade with care, but you must also practice techniques for wielding it most effectively. For example, due to the short blade length of most street-fighting blades, such knives are far better employed primarily for slashing rather than stabbing. Though a spike blade can be used to deliver puncture wounds to the neck, groin, eyes, cheeks, and other vulnerable areas, it is still not as effective in a short-bladed weapon as is a blade which can be used to deliver slashes to the hands and face as well as to the more obvious vulnerable areas. The best combination, of course, is a weapon which allows both slashes and thrusts to be delivered, thereby granting greater versatility.

URBAN SKINNER

My own top choice among close-combat blades for the streets are those from Cold Steel. Although Cold Steel makes at least four excellent street blades, my first choice and most recommended blade is the Urban Skinner. This compact push dagger with a 2-1/4-inch blade is easy to carry on one's person and conforms to the arbitrary 3-inch blade limit on concealed knives enforced by many U.S. police depart-

ments. The Skinner's sheath has a clip which allows it to be worn inside the waistband or elsewhere. I've equipped the inside of one of my jacket pockets with a loop to which I can affix this clip, thus allowing me to keep my hand near the knife while also securing it.

An additional advantage of the Urban Skinner is that even a person not trained in blade usage can wield it effectively by delivering punches and slashes with the fist in a relatively natural manner. An added advantage, especially for women, is that it is very hard to disarm someone who has a push dagger in his fist since he is able to grip it far more tightly than is possible with an average small dagger. The Skinner's blade is also well-designed to deliver either a thrust or a slash, depending on the situation. Although the shape of the Skinner's hilt/handle is well-designed to allow a firm grip, its gripping ability on newer models is additionally enhanced by a hard rubber, checkered grip.

URBAN PAL

A smaller push dagger known as the Urban Pal is also offered by Cold Steel. Only 3-1/8 inches in overall length with a 1-3/4-inch blade, the Urban Pal is fabricated from one piece of steel. It comes with a small sheath affixed to a key chain, thus enhancing the likelihood it will be along if needed. The "Pal'" is so small that it is only useful as a last-ditch weapon; like a razorblade, which has often seen such usage, it can still do a lot of damage to an opponent's face, neck, hands, or other exposed body parts. For normal "urban warfare," however, I would rate the Skinner far superior to the rest.

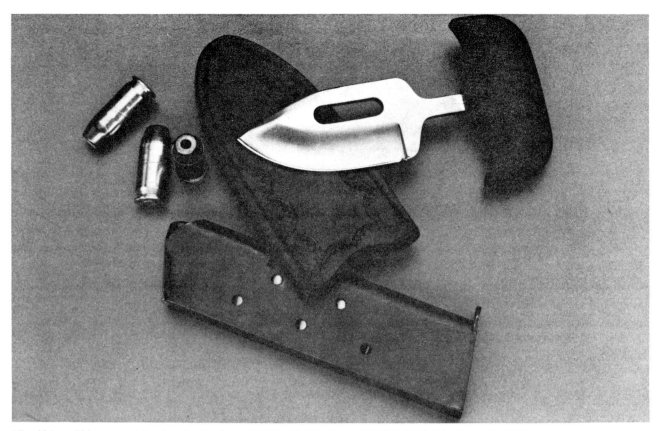

The Urban Skinner and its sheath are shown above. Photo courtesy of Cold Steel.

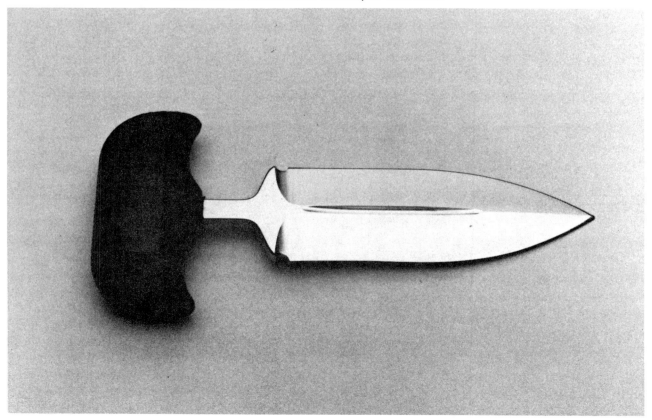

The Terminator is a longer-bladed, double-edged Urban Skinner. Photo courtesy of Cold Steel.

URBAN SHIV AND THE URBAN HUNTER

Two other Cold Steel blades which deserve consideration for urban survival are the Urban Shiv and the Urban Hunter, both of more conventional design with skeletonized hilts. Basically, the only difference between the two knives is in the shapes of their blades. The Urban Shiv has a double-edged, spear-point blade of 2-3/4 inches, while the Urban Hunter has a mini-Bowie blade of 2-3/4 inches. Each comes with a compact sheath which can either be affixed about one's person with a clip or strapped to an arm or leg with a Velcro strap. Each of these knives is fabricated entirely of stainless steel with skeletonized hilts to keep weight down. Still, each hilt is grooved to provide a solid grip and has a thumb rest for proper hand positioning. Personally, I prefer the Shiv to the Hunter, though I've carried both. The Shiv is more effective as a stabbing weapon because of its spear point, though it retains sharpened edges which allow it to be used for slashing as well. The Hunter's edge makes it a more effective slashing weapon; its Bowie-style point is not quite as effective for stabbing. The point can still penetrate quite deeply, however, especially if used for an upward thrust.

I've often carried the Urban Shiv in combination with the Urban Skinner since neither takes up much space about one's person. If carried together, I would normally position the Skinner for use with my left (weak) hand and the Shiv for use with my right (strong) hand.

ADVANTAGES OF COLD STEEL KNIVES

In addition to their effective design and sturdy construction, the Cold Steel line of knives has other advantages which make them a top choice for "urban warfare." First, Cold Steel knives are very reasonably priced, which means that even the person of modest means can be armed with one. Their reasonable price also means that the honest citizen who has just shown a mugger the error of his ways—punctuating his rhetoric with Cold Steel—could easily dispose of the Cold Steel blade if he so desired without being out of pocket for a large amount. Now we all know the "right" thing to do is to report the attempted mugging to the authorities and to take credit for perforating the leaking mugger. However, a lot of citizens also know that our criminal justice system favors the mugger over the muggee defending himself in many urban areas. Therefore, should one desire to surreptitiously dispose of his Cold Steel knife, it bears no serial number and is easily replaced.

TEKNA MICRO KNIFE

Among the other knives specifically marketed for "urban survival" are a group which are not intended to look like knives when carried in a shirt pocket or purse. My personal favorite among these types of blades is the Tekna Micro Knife which masquerades relatively effectively as a pen while carried in the pocket, though even a cursory examination of the implement will identify its true purpose once it's removed from the pocket. My preference for the Micro Knife is based on the sturdiness of its design. Unlike other similar knives in which the blade drops from the hilt in switchblade or gravity knife style, the Micro Knife has a rigidly mounted 2-1/4-inch stiletto blade. To protect and conceal the blade, a shield pulls out of the hilt and covers the blade. Pressing a red button at the top of the hilt/"pen body" retracts this shield and presents the blade for usage. Unlike many of the other knives which masquerade as pens, one gets a sturdy blade with the Micro Knife, one which is unlikely to collapse or break should heavy clothing or bone be encountered. The Micro Knife is not, of course, a heavy-duty fighting knife; rather, it is more of a heavy-duty type than most others of its ilk.

My only objection to my Micro Knife is that it is sometimes a bit difficult to get one's finger positioned correctly over the button to retract the shield prior to bringing the knife into action. If drawn from the pocket and held in the "ice pick" stabbing grip, one can retract the shield quickly and effectively. To retract it from other positions may take multiple attempts. Hence, it is probably best to assume that after drawing the Micro from one's pocket, one retracts the shield—normally as the knife is being swung up into the "ice pick" position—and attempts to immediately deliver a stabbing movement toward the opponent's face or neck. Another reason I favor the Micro Knife over such other

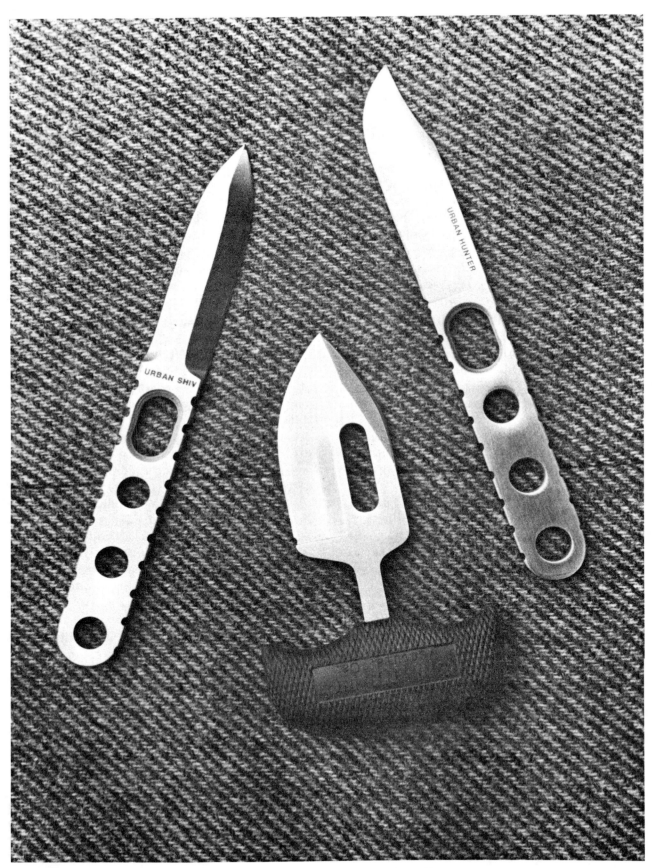

Cold Steel's excellent Urban Skinner is flanked by the Urban Shiv and Urban Hunter.

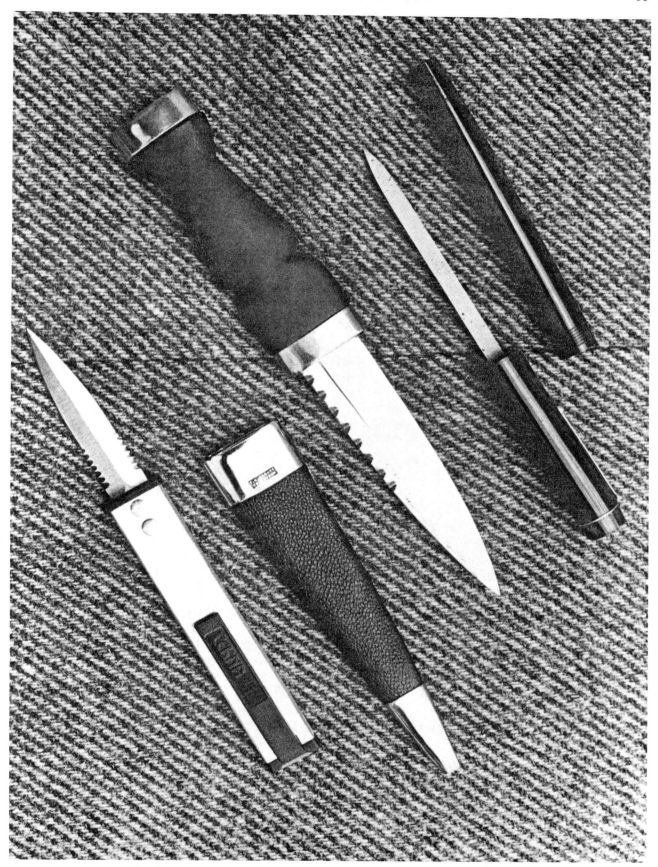

The **Tekna Micro Knife** (left), the author's favorite ''pen'' knife, is shown with a skean dubh and another pen knife.

"pen knives" as the Guardfather, which uses a spike blade, is that the versatile Micro Knife can be used for slashes as well as stabs.

Tekna-Knife and Security Card

Tekna also makes other "urban survival" blades, including the Tekna-Knife and the Tekna Security Card. The Tekna-Knife is similar to the Cold Steel Urban Shiv, being a skeletonized stiletto. The Tekna's blade is slightly longer, however, at 3-1/2 inches, a length that puts it over the legal limit for a concealable knife in many venues. If the Tekna-Knife is chosen, I recommend the one with the matte black finish for more concealability. The Tekna Security Card is a bit of a gimmick since it consists of a blade which slides into a credit-card-sized, black rectangular body. Since far more effective blades can be carried just as easily, I don't recommend the Security Card.

BALI-SONG

There are various types of folding knives which are applicable for street combat, but my own preference is for the Bali-Song butterfly knife. With practice, one can bring this knife into action quickly if so needed. The intimidation value of such quick access implies that you mean business as you flip open the Bali-Song. Intimidation with a knife is not, of course, to be relied upon, but the flash of steel as the Bali-Song opens might discourage a low-grade attacker who lacks superior weaponry. Never, however, try to bluff with a knife! Anyone contemplating close combat with a blade had better be completely serious and realize that such combat is messy—and *very* dangerous. I prefer the clipped-point blade on my Bali-Song since it is primarily a slashing weapon, though its point can be used for thrusting as well. There are some very cheap butterfly knives on the market, though they appear to be functional.

BOOT KNIVES

There is a wide assortment of "boot" knives available as well, though these days most are carried tucked into a waistband or in pockets rather than tucked into the top of a boot. Among the really high-quality ones are the Ran-

dall Guardian and its namesake, the Gerber Guardian, both of which are compact, double-edged, stiletto-type knives with blades of about 4 inches. Each is well-made and durable, with the Gerber being the cheaper of the two since it is mass-produced. Either is effective as a thrusting or stabbing weapon, which can also be used for slashes against unprotected body parts. Each of these blades comes with a compact clip-on holster. Though I like both of these knives and rate them highly for quality and functionality, neither is as good for all-round urban carry as the Urban Shiv because they are bulkier without offering increased effectiveness (except for slightly longer blade length). Still, I recommend either of these blades. The A. G. Russell "Sting" is another excellent blade of this type.

GERBER MARK I

Among the longer blades falling within the general urban combat category is the Gerber Mark I. This knife has a 4-7/8-inch, double-edged stiletto blade and a one-piece hilt and crossguard cast onto the tang. The hilt is roughened to offer a good grip, and the crossguard is slightly hooked to allow it to act as a blade catcher in a blade-to-blade encounter. Held in the standard "knife-fighter's" grip with the thumb on the edge of the crossguard, the Mark I can be used effectively for either thrusting or slashing. It is a well-balanced knife which can even be thrown by a skillful wielder. Its leather sheath has the clip which seems to be standard for "boot" or other concealable knives and uses a quick-release, snap-retaining strap. Although I like the Mark I a lot because of its size, I tend to classify it as a compact fighting knife rather than a real street knife; this doesn't mean that I wouldn't prefer it to one of the smaller blades should I be in a tight situation on the street. Usually, I have chosen the Gerber for street-carry either because I was wearing heavy clothing within which I could conceal it or I carried it along with a compact firearm when wearing "civvies" in a Third World country. I have also included a Mark I in a compact survival kit consisting of a Detonics .45 auto or some other compact handgun, some ammunition, and the Mark I. Normally, this combo has been tucked into the bottom of a briefcase.

The Randall Guardian, though expensive, is an excellent boot knife. The holes in the sheath allow it to be lashed in any convenient location.

Though these Highland regimental skean dubhs are very decorative, they can also serve quite well as fighting knives when correctly used.

SKEAN DUBH

Although its true purpose as a compact fighting knife has been lost since it is now used as a piece of Highland jewelry, the skean dubh is still a reasonably effective urban-combat blade if one bears in mind that the method of mounting the blade into the hilt does not make it a particularly sturdy type of knife. Still, the skean dubh design is such that it can be used effectively for thrusts and slashes at exposed skin surfaces. It also has the advantage of appearing to be an innocuous piece of decoration meant to be worn with the kilt. The presence of a skean dubh among one's effects, especially if one has a Scottish name (such as Thompson), rarely attracts much attention in the United Kingdom, Australia, or Canada, especially if one has a great story ready about it being an heirloom from one's Uncle Angus who carried it throughout the Great War.

CIA LETTER OPENERS

One final group of urban fighting knives which should be mentioned are the nylon/fiberglass blades which bill themselves as "CIA Letter Openers." Theoretically, the appeal of these blades is that they will pass through airport security checks and other metal detectors. I assume the idea is also that they will seem to be less of a "weapon" should one be found carrying one. In practice, however, most law-enforcement agencies would still probably treat them as "dangerous and deadly weapons." Therefore, I would normally choose one of the other blades mentioned for "covert" carry.

Most of the blades discussed in this chapter are designed specifically as close-quarters defensive weapons meant to be concealed about one's person. As a result, they represent a trade-off between effectiveness and compactness. It is possible to find a concealable blade which can still be wielded with a devastating effect, but one will have to know how to use such a weapon and have the willingness to get very messy in the process. Larger blades—up to machetes—have been carried concealed and used for urban combat and will be in the future, but they are not designed specifically with street fighting in mind and, therefore, do not fall within the scope of this chapter.

Appendix:
Knife Makers

Al Mar Knives
5755 Jean Rd. Suite 101
Lake Oswego, OR 97034

Applegate-Fairbairn
Box 22B
Scottsburg, OR 97473

Atlanta Cutlery
Box 839
Conyers, GA 30207

Bali-Song
3039 Roswell St.
Los Angeles, CA 90065

Brigade Quartermasters
266 Roswell St.
Marietta, GA 30060
   (Victorinox, Spanish Army Knives, etc.)

Buck Knives
P.O. Box 1267
El Cajon, CA 92022

Camillus Cutlery Co.
52-54 W. Genesee St.
Camillus, NY 13030

Cold Steel
2128 Unit D, Knoll Drive
Ventura, CA 93003

Gerber Legendary Blades
14200 S.W. 72nd St.
Portland, OR 97223

Gutmann Cutlery, Inc.
900 South Columbus Ave.
Mt. Vernon, NY 10550
   (Importers of the Brewer Explorer)

Gil Hibben
2703 Costigan Way
Louisville, KY 40220

Ka-Bar Cutlery Inc.
5777 Grant Ave.
Cleveland, OH 44105

Lifeknife
Box 771
Santa Monica, CA 90406

Jimmy Lile
Rt. 1
Russelville, AR 72801

Randall Made Knives
Box 1988
Orlando, FL 32802

RP Custom Knives
1922 Spartanburg Hwy.
Hendersonville, NC 28739

A. G. Russell
1705 Hwy. 71N
Springdale, AR 72764

Survival Equipment Ltd.
Chandos House
42 St. Owens St.
Hereford
England
   (ACE-PAL-O Universal Survival Knife)

A. Daniel Valois
Rt. 2, Box 339
Orefield, PA 18069

J. Wiseman
22 Lanland Dr.
Whitecross, Hereford
England HR4 OQG
   (Mini-survival [prepacked] kit)